Alfred Burton

Rush-Bearing

an account of the old custom of strewing rushes, carrying rushes to church, the rush-cart, garlands in churches, morris-dancers, the wakes and the rush

Alfred Burton

Rush-Bearing

an account of the old custom of strewing rushes, carrying rushes to church, the rush-cart, garlands in churches, morris-dancers, the wakes and the rush

ISBN/EAN: 9783337264178

Printed in Europe, USA, Canada, Australia, Japan

Cover: Foto ©Andreas Hilbeck / pixelio.de

More available books at **www.hansebooks.com**

Of this Work only Five Hundred Copies
are issued, of which this is

No.

Rush-Bearing:

AN ACCOUNT OF THE OLD CUSTOM OF STREWING RUSHES;
CARRYING RUSHES TO CHURCH; THE RUSH-CART;
GARLANDS IN CHURCHES; MORRIS-DANCERS;
THE WAKES; THE RUSH.

BY

ALFRED BURTON.

"Many precious rites and customs of our rural ancestry are gone, or stealing from us."
Wordsworth.

MANCHESTER: BROOK & CHRYSTAL.
1891.

Contents.

	PAGE
RUSH-STREWING IN HOUSES,	1
RUSH-STREWING IN CHURCHES,	13
CARRYING RUSHES TO CHURCH,	24
THE RUSH-CART,	39
GARLANDS IN CHURCHES,	89
THE MORRIS-DANCERS,	95
THE WAKES,	147
THE RUSH,	166
INDEX,	183
LIST OF SUBSCRIBERS,	185

Introduction.

MANY of our old customs are fading away into the dim mists of antiquity, and all but the name will soon be forgotten. This is much to be regretted, because they were attended with a great deal of pure enjoyment, and were looked forward to by the people for weeks before the event. One of these is the old custom of strewing rushes, and its attendant ceremony of the rush-bearing, with its quaint rush-cart and fantastic morris-dancers. Once common to the whole country, it now lingers only in a few isolated places, principally in the hill districts of Lancashire and Yorkshire. Many scattered notices of the custom occur, but no general description, and it would therefore seem that the time has come when some effort should be made to place on record what is known, before the knowledge of it fades from the recollection of the passing generation, to illustrate the subject with such views as actual representations of existing specimens afford, before the custom itself becomes obsolete, and, "like an unsubstantial pageant faded," leaves not a trace behind. Although a dozen or more rush-carts could be met with twenty-five years ago, now the country has to be ransacked to find one, and that a mere caricature of the once well-built, well-dressed cart of former times, accompanied by a few young men whose attempts to dance the morris show how rapidly it is being forgotten.

In the following pages no attempt has been made to write a high-flown imaginary description of a picturesque pageant, but to give such reliable historical information as can be obtained, supplemented by descriptions of the custom as practised in various parts of the country, and existing instances. The illustrations, it is believed, will give a good idea of its main features, and serve to show the succeeding generation how their ancestors turned simple customs into amusement, enjoyment, and a general periodical holiday.

The saying,

> "By many strokes the work is done
> That could not be performed by one,"

is as applicable to book-writing as house-building, and as the following work, some of the materials for which have been gathered nearly twenty years, has been principally compiled (for in the nature of such a work a compilation it must necessarily be) during the intervals of a long and, at times, severe illness, I must confess it does not come up to the standard I had set before me, but failing health warns me that I had better place on record such information as I had already got rather than run the risk of losing the whole by striving to complete an ideally perfect whole. I have to thank Mr. W. H. Allmit, of the Bodleian Library, Oxford, for quotations I could not obtain in Manchester; to Mr. J. J. Alexander, of 78, King Street, Manchester, I am indebted for much assistance in obtaining some of the illustrations, verifying references, etc.; to Mr. William Andrews, F.R.H.S., Secretary of the Hull Literary Club, I am under many obligations, as well as for the loan of "A Lancashire Rush-cart," which appeared in his valuable "Curiosities of the Church," and whose "Old-time Punishments," just published, bids fair to surpass it. To Mr. Morgan Brierley, of Denshaw House, I am obliged for notices of the custom in his neighbourhood. Mr. J. Lawton, of St. Chad's, Saddleworth, willingly allowed me to reproduce his picture of "Saddleworth Rush-bearing." For the beautiful plate of the "Rush-bearing at Borrowdale," I am indebted to the late Llewellynn

Jewitt, F.S.A. Mr. T. Oliver, artist, of 8, King Street, Manchester, has rendered me great assistance with his pencil, and considerably enriched these pages. Mr. C. W. Sutton, of the Free Reference Library, Manchester, has afforded me much help in my researches there. Lastly, to Messrs. W. & R. Chambers, Messrs. Chatto & Windus, the proprietors of the "Art Journal" and "The Graphic," I am indebted for permission to use illustrations which have appeared in their works, and which are duly set forth in the text.

ALFRED BURTON.

OCTOBER, 1890.

RUSH-BEARING.

Rush-strewing in Houses.

IN former times the floors of houses were composed of nothing more than the earth, well beaten and smoothed; those of the better sort were usually paved with tiles or flags, and very little care appears to have been bestowed upon cleanliness, as far as the floor was concerned, except that it was occasionally strewn with fresh rushes, sometimes, as a refinement, mixed with sweet herbs and flowers. In Thos. Newton's "Herball to the Bible," 1587: "Sedge and rushes, with the which many in the country do use in Sommer time to strawe their parlours and churches, as well for cooleness as for pleasant smell" are mentioned. The species preferred was the *Calamus aromaticus*, which, when bruised, gives forth an odour resembling that of the myrtle; in its absence, inferior kinds were used. Even the palaces of royalty were frequently strewn with rushes, straw, or hay. William the Conqueror granted certain lands at Aylesbury to one of his followers on condition of " Finding straw for the bed of our lord the king, and to straw his chamber, and by paying three eels to our lord the king when he should come to Aylesbury in winter. And also finding for the king, when he should come to Aylesbury in summer, straw for his bed, and, moreover, grass or rushes to strew his chamber, and also paying two green geese; and these services aforesaid he was to perform thrice a year, if the king should happen to come three times to Aylesbury, and not oftener." *

King John, in 1207, slept at the house of Robert de Leveland, at Westminster; and the Barons of the Exchequer were directed to pay for the straw bought on account of the visit of the king. A charge was made in the "Household Roll of Edward II." for John de Carleford making a journey from York to Newcastle, for a supply of rushes for strewing the king's chamber; and according to the "Household Book of Edward IV." the groom of the chamber was to bring daily "rushes and litter for the paylettes all the year." † In many of the larger manor-houses an officer, termed the "rush-strewer," was kept, whose duty it was to keep the hall floor duly supplied with fresh rushes. "LVI. The proper officers are, between six and seven o'clock in the morning, to make the fire in and *straw* the King's privy chamber." ‡ Some old houses had the lower part of the door cut away to admit of the rushes for the floor extending to the threshold, the latter being raised a few inches to prevent the wind from rushing in at the opening thus made.

The vast number of rushes brought into London for the purpose of strewing the floors became such a nuisance that as early as 1416 it had been ordered that all rushes laden in boats or skiffs, and brought to London for sale, should be sold by the cartload, and made up in the boats, not on the wharves near the Thames, under a heavy penalty; and again, in 1419, "that the rishbotes at the Flete and elsewhere in London should be taken into the hands of the Chamberlain, and the Chamberlain should cause all the streets to be

---
* See Blount's "Tenures of Land," 1679.
† Parker's "Ancient Domestic Architecture," 1853, vol. 2, p. 101.
‡ "Household Orders of Henry VIII."

cleansed." * " Green rushes, O," was long one of the cries of London, but is now remembered only in a song. John Lydgate, a monk of Bury St. Edmunds, who wrote, about the middle of the 15th century, a quaint old ballad called "London Lyckpenny," or Lackpenny, says that in his peregrinations "One cryde mackerell, ryster [rushes] grene, an other gan greete;" and in a small folio collection of London Street Cries now in the British Museum, supposed to be of the time of Charles II., " Buy any Russes?" occurs. These rushes were used for strewing on the floors of the houses of the citizens.

Sir Thomas More (1483) describes Elizabeth, the widowed Queen of Edward IV., when in the Sanctuary at Westminster, as "sitting alone amongst the *Rushes* in her grief and distress."

At the christening of the Lady Elizabeth, 25 Henry VIII. (1533-4), "all the walles betwene the King's Place and the Fryars were hanged with Arras, and all the way *strewed with rushes*."†

In a MS. account of the submission of Shane O'Neale, on Twelfth Day, 4 Elizabeth (1562), preserved in the Carew MS. in the Archiepiscopal Library at Lambeth Palace, mention is made of the creation as earl of Con O'Neale, 34 Henry VIII. (1542-3). The account of the ceremony states that "ffirst the Queenes closett at Greenwiche was richlie hanged w^t cloth of Arras and *well strewed w^t rushes*."

Queen Elizabeth appears to have been the last monarch whose palace was strewn with rushes. In the description of an interview with the Queen at the palace of Placentia, Greenwich, in 1598, which appears in the travels of Paul Hentzner, a German, it is stated: " We were admitted, by an order Mr. Rogers had procured from the Lord Chamberlain, into the presence-

* Govett's "King's Book of Sports," 1890, p. 50.
† Harl. MSS., 1107.

chamber, hung with rich tapestry, and the floor after the English fashion *strewed with hay* (rushes), through which the Queen commonly passes in her way to the chapel." *

"When Henry III., King of France, demanded of Monsieur Dandelot what especial things he had noted in England during the time of his negotiation there, he answered that he had seen but three things remarkable, which were, that the people did drinke in bootes, eate rawe fish, and *strewed all their best roomes with hay;* meaning blacke jacks, oysters, and rushes." †

"The strewing of rushes when guests were expected was deemed a token of respect. The wits of the Elizabethan age had an old saying, to the effect that many strewed green rushes for a stranger who would not give one to a friend. It was deemed an act of politeness to cover the floor with fresh rushes for a guest, and if this were not done the host was said not to care a rush for him." ‡

"Strangers have green rushes, when daily guests
Are not worth a rush."
—*Lily*, "*Sappho and Phao.*"

It is true that in the romance of "Twaine and Gawin" we read:

"When he unto chamber yede,
The chamber flore, and als ye beds,
With klathes of gold were al over spred;"

but although floor carpets were sometimes used in the chambers, this was uncommon, and they seem to have been more usually, like the hall, strewed with rushes. It appears that sometimes, as a refinement in gaiety, flowers were mixed with the rushes. In a fabliau in Meon (1, 75), a lady, who expects her lover, lights a

* Bayley's "Graphic and Historical Illustrator," 1834, p. 199.
† "Wits, Fits, and Fancies," 4to, 1614.
‡ Andrews' "Curiosities of the Church," 1890, p. 54.

fire in the chamber, and spreads rushes and flowers on the floor:

> "Vient á l'ostel, lo feu esclaire,
> Jons et flors espandre par l'aire." *

Bradshaw, in his "Life of St. Werburgh" (1500), writes:

> "All Herbes and flowres fragrant, fayre and swete
> Were strewed in halls, and layed under theyre fete."

Froissart, relating the death of Gaston, Count de Foix, says that the count went to his chamber, which he found ready strewed with rushes and green leaves, and the walls were hung with boughs, newly cut, for perfume and coolness, as the weather was marvellously hot. Adam Davie, Marshall of Stratford-le-Bow, who wrote about the year 1312, in his poem of the "Life of Alexander," describing the marriage of Cleopatra, says:

> "There was many a blithe grome;
> Of olive, and of ruge floures,
> Weren y strewed halls and bowres;
> With samytes and bawdekyns,
> Weren curtayned the gardyns."

Frequent references occur in the works of the old dramatists to the custom of freshly strewing rushes for a guest. In the "Taming of the Shrew" Grumio asks:

> "Is the supper ready, the house trimm'd,
> rushes strew'd, cobwebs swept?"

and in "Katherine and Petruchio," Act IV., Scene 1, it is asked:

> "Are the rushes strewn?"

In the old play of the "Two Noble Kinsmen," the gaoler's daughter is represented carrying "strewings

---

* Wright's "History of Domestic Manners and Sentiments," 1862, p. 246.

for the two prisoners' chambers." Again, in Beaumont and Fletcher's "Valentinian," II., 4:

> "Where is this stranger? Rushes, ladies, rushes,
> Rushes as green as summer for this stranger."

Heywood's "Dialogue," etc. (1576), also has "To strew green rushes for a stranger;" and Hazlitt[*] says the saying is still current in Cornwall.

The custom of strewing rushes in the way where processions were to pass is attributed by poets to all times and all countries. Shakespeare alludes to it at the coronation of Henry; when the procession is returning the grooms cry:

> "More rushes, more rushes!"
> —*Henry IV., Act V., Sc. 5.*

Braithwaite's "Strappado for the Divell," (1615), has:

> "All haile to Hymen and his Marriage Day!
> Strew Rushes, and quickly come away;
> Strew Rushes, Maides, and ever as you strew,
> Think one day, Maides, like will be done for you."

William Browne, in his "Britannia's Pastorals" (1625), I., 2, in a description of a wedding, writes:

> "Full many maids, clad in their best array,
> In honour of the bride, come with their flaskets
> Fill'd full with flowers: others in wicker baskets
> Bring forth the marish rushes, to o'erspread
> The ground whereon to church the lovers tread."

A correspondent, writing to the "Gentleman's Magazine,"[†] in 1782, says that in "riding through Abingdon, in Berks, early on one of the first Sundays in October, I found the people in the street at the entrance of the town very busy in adorning the outside of their houses with boughs of trees and garlands of

---

[*] "English Proverbs and Proverbial Phrases," 1882, p. 359.
[†] Vol. 52, p. 558.

flowers, and the paths were strewed with rushes. One
house was distinguished by a greater number of garlands than the rest, and some were making to be fixed
at the ends of poles. On enquiring the reason, I was
told that it was usual to have this ceremony performed
in the street in which the new mayor lived, on the first
Sunday that he went to church after his election."
This custom has long ceased in Abingdon.

At York, on the Friday after Corpus Christi Day,
the clergy and corporation, bearing banners and lighted
torches, perambulated the streets, the houses being
decorated with tapestry and other hangings, and the
road strewed with rushes and flowers.

The straw and rushes were often allowed to accumulate in the houses until they became rotten and offensive, a fresh strewing serving to hide the filth beneath.
Noblemen were in the habit of removing from one
dwelling to another whilst the house was cleansed;
whilst the lesser gentry frequently erected bowers in
the summer whilst the rushes in the hall were turned
out. An old author, writing in 1511, thus speaks of a
custom which existed on "God's son-daye," or Easter
Day: "Ye know well that it is the maner at this daye
to do the fire out of the hall, and the black wynter
brondes, and all things that is foule with fume and
smoke shall be done awaye; and there the fire was
shall be gayly arrayed with fayre flowres, and strewed
with green ryshes all about." This process was termed
"going to sweeten." The most pitiful complaints were
made by Lord Paget to Edward VI.'s privy council,
because, being in disgrace, he was confined to Beau-
desert, which, he assured them, "though pretty, was
too small, and had withal become, by some months'
residence, horribly unsavoury, and could not be sweet-
ened without the removal of his family."* The refined
feelings of Thomas á Beckett prompted him to keep

---

* Miss Strickland's "Lives of the Queens of England," 1842, vol. 5, p. 424.

his house in a clean and tasteful state: "for his Hall was every daye in Somer season strewed with grene Russhes, and in Wynter with clene Hey, for to save the Knyghtes' clothes that sate on the Flore for defaute of place to syt on." * The author of the "Life of Olaus Tryggv," speaking of Thorleifer, one of the Yule guests of Haquin, Earl of Norway, says:

"Selst han nidr ietarliga i halmimr,"
(He sat down on the last straw),

an expression which, however, might seem to imply the use of bundles of straw, as the primitive predecessors of a more artificial convenience for repose, were it not otherwise proved to be the practice to employ straw as a covering for the floors. † It was thought to be a piece of unnecessary luxury on the part of Wolsey when he wisely caused the rushes at Hampton Court to be changed every day.

In the time of Queen Mary the floor was neither swept nor washed, but received a fresh strewing of rushes, which accumulated layer above layer, mixed with the bones and droppings from the table. Erasmus, in a letter to Dr. Francis, physician to Cardinal Wolsey, describing the interior of common dwellings in the reign of Henry VIII., says:

"As to the floors, they are usually made of clay, covered with rushes that grow in fens, which are so slightly removed now and then that the lower part remains sometimes for twenty years together, and in it a collection of filthiness not to be named. Hence, upon a change of weather, a vapour is exhaled, very pernicious, in my opinion, to the human body. I am persuaded it would be far more healthful if the use of these rushes were quite laid aside, and the chambers so built as to let in the air on two or three sides, with such glass windows as might either be thrown quite open or kept quite shut, without small crannies to let in the wind, for as it is useful sometimes to admit a free air, so it is sometimes to exclude it."

* "The Festyvall," 1528.
† Hampson's "Medii Ævi Kalendarium," 1841, vol. i, p. 340.

When room was required for dancing:

"To mince it with a mission, tracying a pavion or galliardo uppon the rushes,"*

a circle was swept clear in the centre of the hall floor, a custom mentioned by the early dramatists in the call of "a hall, a hall." Shakespeare, in "Romeo and Juliet," Act I., Sc. 5:

"*A hall! a hall!* give room, and foot it girls;"

and in Nicholas Brereton's "Workes of a Young Wit," 1577:

"And then *a hall*, for dancers must have room."

Marston, in his "Scourge of Villanie," 1599, 8vo, also says:

"A hall, a hall;
Roome for the spheres, the Orbes Celestiall
Will daunce Kempe's Jigg."

Shakespeare has several allusions to the custom of strewing rushes on the floor:

"Let wantons, light of heart,
Tickle the senseless rushes with their feet."
—*Romeo and Juliet, Act I., Sc. 4.*

He also tells us how Tarquin

"being lighted, by the light he spies
Lucretia's glove, wherein her needle sticks,
He takes it from *the rushes* where it lies."
—*Rape of Lucrece, 1594.*

and again, in "Cymbeline," Act II., Sc. 2:

"Our Tarquin thus
Did softly press *the rushes*, ere he wakened
The chastity he wounded."

* "Riche his Farewell," 1581.

In Ben Jonson's "Every Man out of his Humour,"
(III, 9) we find:

"Sweet lady, I do honour the meanest rush in this chamber
for your love:"

but a contrary sentiment is in the "Dumb Knight,"
(O. Pl., IV., 475):

"Thou dancest on my heart, lascivious queen,
 Ev'n as upon these *rushes* which thou treadest."

A remarkable proof of the custom of laying rushes on the floor is contained in a manuscript "History of a moste horrible Murder comyttyd at Fevershame in Kente," in the reign of Edward VI., 1550. The assassins, having strangled and stabbed Master Arden, "toke a clowt and wyped where it was blowdy, and *strewyd agayne ye rushes* that were shuffled wth strugglinge." The rushes were among the means which led to the detection and conviction of the murderers. The mayor of Feversham and some of the townsmen discovered the body in a field, and "than they lokynge about hym, found some *rushes of ye parlour* stickynge in his slippars," whence they concluded that he had been slain in a house, and not where the body was discovered." *

In August, 1600, an attempt was made to assassinate James VI. of Scotland, at Gowrie House. After the affray one of the gentlemen who had accompanied the king "found a silk garter lying among the *bent* or rough grass with which the floor of the round chamber was covered." †

The practice of strewing rushes on the floors in private houses is noticed by Dr. Johnson from "Caius de Ephemera Britannica." It was extremely widespread, and is mentioned in Weinhold's "Die Deutschen

---

* Harl. MSS., 542, fo. 31, 376.
† Tytler's "History of Scotland," 8vo edition, 1879, vol. 4, p. 296, col. 1.

Frauen in Mittelalter," Wien, 1851, p. 340. Liebricht, in his "Gervase of Tilbury," 1856, p. 60, advances the conjecture that this custom is probably a remnant of some heathen rite, and this supposition is confirmed by an observation of A. D. Kuhn, in his "Westphäl Sagen," etc., Leipsic, 1859, vol. II., p. 110, in reference to an old Hindoo custom. Swift also remarks on the practice in the "Polite Conversations," dialogue 1.*

The strewing of rushes in houses is now obsolete, though the custom lingered on till well in the present century. I remember one old farmhouse in Cheshire, where, twenty-five years ago, the parlour, which had a flagged floor, was strewn on the 1st of May with green rushes, over which sprigs of lavender and rosemary were scattered. The huge fireplace was filled with green boughs, stuck in jugs, and plants, the old room having a most refreshing smell on being entered.

Mr. William Andrews informs me that the custom of strewing the floors with rushes is still practised at the Hull Trinity House. No date is fixed for the removal of the old rushes and the strewing of fresh ones, which takes place as often as the rushes are dirty, and there is no ceremony attending it.

Hone, in his "Year Book," p. 725, speaks of the boarded floor of Trinity House, Deptford, being strewed with green rushes on the occasion of the visit of the Brethren of Trinity House, during the fair in 1825. The town hall at Liskeard, in Cornwall, was strewed with rushes on particular occasions, as late as 1842.

The English stage was strewed with rushes in Shakespeare's time;† and the Globe Theatre was roofed with rushes, or as Taylor, the "water-poet,"

* "Works," London, 1801, vol. 1, p. 280.
† Reed's "Shakspere," vol. 9., p 331.

describes it, the old theatre "had a thatched hide," and it was through the rushes in the roof taking fire that the first Globe Theatre was burnt down. Killigrew told Pepys, in 1667, how he had improved the stage from a time when there was "nothing but rushes upon the ground, and everything else mean." To the rushes succeeded matting.

Rush-strewing in Churches.

SEATS were not provided in churches until the fifteenth century, and the floors being flagged made the feet of the worshippers excessively cold after long standing, particularly in winter. Much kneeling, also, was required by the service, and some softer material became necessary, as cushions could only be provided by the most wealthy. The material found most suitable in the dwellings of the people was equally available for use in the church, and rushes were used as a covering for the floor from a very early period.

The Tailors' Guild at Salisbury was under the patronage of St. John; wherefore, they decreed "that the two stewardis for the time being, every yere, shall make and sette afore Seynt John ye Baptist, upon the awter, two tapers of one lb of wex, and a garland of Roses, to be sette upon Seynt John's hed, and that the chaple be strewed with green rushes."*

In Harl. MSS., 2103, fo. 81, is an order by the visitors deputed by the Archbishop of York to enquire into the state of the church of St. Oswald, Chester, and its fitness for the celebration of divine service:

"27 August, 1633, . . . upon a diligent view taken by the said commissioners of the said church of St. Oswald, it did appear unto them that the said church was very undecent and unseemely, the stalls thereof being patched and peeced, and some broken, and some higher than other; and that the said church was much defiled with *rushes* and other filthiness, The said commissioners did order and

* Friend's "Flowers and Flower Lore," 1886, p. 600.

enjoyne the said churchwardens to cause the rushes and other filthiness forthwth to bee taken out of the same church ... and that the same Stalls should bee decently flagged or boarded over."

The church at Kirkham, Lancashire, was flagged 24th July, 1634; and in 1781 wood forms, instead of rushes, were put into the church to kneel upon. At Saddleworth the church floor was covered with these substitutes for flags and matting till the year 1826, when the church was paved for the first time. Bishop Law visited that curious fabric a few years prior to that time, and on seeing the rushes spread over the floor said, "I would not lodge my horse in this place,"—a remark which was keenly felt by the churchwardens.* The first wooden floor was of boards, two inches thick and eighteen inches wide, laid on oak sleepers, to which, however, they were not attached either by pegs or nails, resting by their weight. It was removed about seventeen years ago. Down to the year 1820, the floor of Castleton Church, Derbyshire, was unpaved, and covered with rushes. The floor of Pilling Church, Lancashire, was covered with rushes till about the year 1868.

Heybridge Church, near Maldon, Essex, was formerly strewn with rushes; and round the pews, in holes made apparently for the purpose, were placed small twigs just budding.†

The custom of taking these rushes to church gradually developed into a religious festival, and although some writers deny that there is any connection between the rush-bearing and the wakes, or feast of the dedication of the church to some saint, the evidence is overwhelming that the custom of annually renewing the rushes did take place at that time, for although instances occur in which the rush-bearing, and also the wakes, do take place at a different time to the saint's

---
* Raines MSS. (Chetham Library, Manchester), vol. 1, p. 165.
† "Notes and Queries," 2nd series, vol. 1, p. 471.

day to whom the church is dedicated, yet it should be remembered that some wakes have been altered for local reasons. It is said of one village in Cheshire that the clerk gave out in the churchyard: "Th' wakes will not be held till th' week after next, as farmer———has not got in his hay;" and this postponement till a day more convenient to the parishioners has taken place in more than one instance. On one occasion, William Shawcross, of the "George and Dragon" Inn, Gorton, altered the wakes until Eccles wakes Sunday, when, consequently, few strangers visited Gorton, to the no small chagrin of the wakes ruler, who declared that henceforth, "let what come go," he would never interfere with the wakes time again. In March, 1884, an agitation was got up in Stockport in favour of holding the wakes on an early day in August instead of the end of September. In 1885 both dates were kept; but though the battle of the wakes raged for two or three years the old one won the day, the people preferring the "old original." At Disley, in Cheshire, the wakes is said to have been formerly held after the *first fall of snow*.

As the wake was a religious festival, always commencing on Sunday, fresh rushes would be deemed necessary for the occasion. The getting of the rushes at such a time and bearing them to church would naturally lead to some drinking and merrymaking; rivalry between the various townships in a parish would take place, and so the bundle of rushes would come to be decorated, the cart containing the rushes made ornamental, garlands of flowers obtained to decorate the church, till the rush-bearing at last became a picturesque spectacle.

The rushes for the church were provided at the cost of the parishioners, at the instance of the churchwardens; and where there were more than one township in the parish, each took it in turn for one year at its own cost, as a difficulty sometimes arose as to the proportion to be borne by each township when done collectively. At Newton Chapel, near Manchester, the flooring being of clay, the pews were well carpeted with rushes, which were yearly renewed by each township in its turn, at the wakes. These were Newton, Failsworth, Moston, and Droylsden, but the latter has ceased to attend, having now a church of its own, and also holds its wakes at a different time to the other three. In the Churchwardens' Accounts of Padiham, under date 18 May, 1730, there is a

"Mem'dm.—That it was then agreed that the Inhabitants of each Township or Liberty contributing to bringing Rishes to the Church or Chappell of Padiham, each place bringing Rishes once in four years respectively for that particular place, shall bear the Charges of the Rishes bringing without charging the other Towns.
Witness our
"Hen. Kirkham,   Tho. Whitaker,
John Bridge,   R. Webster,
John Hitchon,   Lra. Pollard,
William Robinson, John Whitehead."

Du Cange explains "Juncare—locum floribus vel juncis spargere. Juncus, majoribus festis sparsus in ecclesia et alibi. Consuetudines MSS. Sancti Augustini Lemovicensis: 'In festo Augustinii . . . præpositus debet recipere *juncum, qui debetur ex consuetudine* ad parandum chorum et capitulum.'" Here was clearly, in this case, an obligation, derived from long usage, on the neighbouring farms and farmers to bring in contributions of freshly-cut rushes for the festival of the local saint.

At the bishop's visitation, 23rd October, 1622, Robert Aughton, of Penwortham, was presented as contumacious "for not bearing Rushes with his towne to the churche."* On the 26th September, 1623, John Bell, Henry Knowle, Henry Walker, and Richard

* Raines MSS., vol. 22, p. 190.

Birches, the churchwardens of Garstang, were summoned before the bishop on the charge of having warned the parishioners (under a penalty of ten groats a household) to bring rushes to the church on the Sunday, whereas St. James' Day was the day of rushbearing appointed by the bishop. They had also neglected to "decently flag the church," and had failed to provide bread and wine according to the canon.*

The sexton, as a rule, was the person who had to see to the cleansing of the church of the old rushes. In 1681, 10s. per annum additional was allowed to Thomas Bishop, the sexton at Kirkham, for bringing rushes into the church; and in the Churchwardens' Accounts, Padiham, 5 June, 1652, there is a regulation for this work being done:

"It was thought fitt and agreed by ye Inhabitants of ye P'sh church of Padiham that whosoever recyveth ye some of 6s. yearly for sweepinge ye Alleys in church & that shall receive 2s. yearly for clensinge ye church of ould rushes & Sweepinge against new rushes come in shall do it duely, viz, ye Alleys weekly and also ye gutters of ye church & ye pypes of lead to be clensed as often as neede shall requyre."

There is also an entry in the Frodsham Town Accounts:

"1630. Paid to Robert Raborne for getting out the old rushes of the church, oo „ oo „ viijd."

The Churchwardens' Accounts at Burnley contain several items for cleansing the church and getting out old rushes:

```
"1733-4. Paid Barnes [the sexton] for dressing
         the church at the Rushburying  -    -   0  1  0
 1734-5. Paid do. for dressing Church at
         Rushbearing    -      -      -     -   0  1  0
 1754.   Sexton dressing rushes out    -     -   0  1  0
 1760-1. To cleansing church at Rushbearing-     0  1  0
 1778.   To William Parker for carrying a Cart
         load of Rushes into Church     -    -   0  1  0."
```

* Fishwick's "History of Garstang," 1877-9, pp. 272-3.

Du Cange notices the custom, and cites a monastic manuscript in which it is stated that the almoner was bound to find rushes for the choir and cloister on the greater festivals.*

The following extracts from various Churchwardens' Accounts show not only the antiquity but the prevalence of the custom all over the country :—

"1408. For one trusse of stree   -   -   -   vid.
1427. For rushes at Easter   -   -   -   vid.
  ,,   For straw at Chrystmas   -   -   -   ixd.
1599. Payd for rosmarye and bayes ye whole yeare † 1s. vid.
  ,,   For a load of green rushes   -   -   -   viiid.
1638. Payde the Clarke for strewings at Christmas   1s.
                                          —*All Saints', Bristol.*

1493. For 3 Burdens of rushes for ye new pews   -   3d.
1504. Paid for 2 Berden Rysshes for the strewing
        the newe pewes   -   -   -   3d.
                                      —*St. Mary-at-Hill, London.*

1515. Paid for twelve burden of rushes for the
        White Hall   -   -   -   13s.
1544. Paid for rushes against the dedication day,
        which is always the 1st Sunday in October   1s. 5d.
                                      —*St. Margaret's, Westminster.*

1546. For rysshes in festo Pasce   -   -   -   iiijd.
  ,, ,, ryngyng at Ester   -   -   -   viijd.
  ,, ,, rysshes at Wytsontyd   -   -   -   vjd.
  ,, ,, ,,   ,, Mydsomer   -   -   -   viijd.
1551. ,, rushyes in festo omn' sanctor'   -   -   vjd.
1552. ,, russhes against All Hallowtyde   -   -   xd.
  ,, ,, ryngyng on All Hallow's nyght   -   -   xvjd.

(These entries are in every instance associated with charges for ringing the Cathedral Bells.)

1584. To Edward Griffith for boughs, rishes, and
        other thinges, at what time the Earle of
        Leicester came hither   -   -   xviijs. ijd.
                              —*Treasurer's Accounts, Chester Cathedral.*

* Glossary in voc. "Juncus."

† These were probably to strew in the church on days of Humiliation and Thanksgiving, when it was the custom to strew churches with herbs and flowers. The Greeks have a custom at the present day of strewing the floors of their churches with sprigs of myrtle, which give a peculiar crispness and freshness to the atmosphere.

"1595. Gave for wine to the Rushbearers - 3s. 8d.
1599. Gave for wine to those who brought
       Rushes from Buglawton to our chapel   3s. 0d.
1607. To the Rushbearers, wine, ale, & cakes - 6s. 0d.
              —*Congleton Town Accounts.*

1623. Item, spent at the Rushbearinge -   viijd.
1626. Item, spent in fetchinge in Bybles, and at
       the Rushbearinge - - -   xijd.
              —*Churchwardens' Accounts, Prestbury.*

1767. Oct. 22. P'd. to the Rush Cart - 0 2 6d.
1785. Paid Cart load of Rushes - - 0 6 0
              —*Rosthorne.*

1621. Paid for dressinge the church against the
       Rushbearinge - - -   ijs.
1625. Paid for sweeping and rubbing the pues
       and formes in the church - - iijs. iiijd.
1661. Paid for getting forth of all the mats,
       rushes, and makinge the church cleane
       against the Rushbearinge - -   3s. 0d.
1663. Spent the 15th day of August in attending
       to see good order at the Rushbearinge   4d.
1670. Paid for moeing and getting of Rushes to
       dress the church - - - 1s. 0d.
  „   Paid for sweeping the Church before the
       Rushbearing - - -   2s. 0d.
1679. Spent on ye Rushbearing on those which
       come to prevent disorder in the church   2s. 0d.
1685. Paid for the Rushbearing, of the Parish-
       ioners and others for their pains -   7s. 6d.
              —*Wilmslow.*

1603. Rushes to strew the church - - ixs. vjd.
1632. Paid for perfuming the church -   xxxs.
  „   „   „ carrying the rushes out of the
       church in the sickness time - -   vs.
1776. Paid to the sexton for rushing the church   xs.
              —*Town Accounts, Kirkham.*

       Item, Pd. Clarke for sweeping church,
        getting out Rushes, &c. - - 00 10 10d.
1642. Paid for getting out Rishes and sweep-
       ing Church - - - 00 05 00d.
1649. ffor ringynge on the Rushberinge day - 00 01 00

"1657. A shilling disallowed
1717. Pd. Saxon for carrying Rushes into
       church   -   -   -   -   00 01 00
                        —*Churchwardens' Accounts, Rochdale.*

1749. Pd. at rush cart for ale   -   -   1s. 8d.
                                            —*Castleton.*

1768-9. Paid to the Rush Cart   -   -   2s. 6d.
1769.   Forr the rush cart   -   -   -   2s. 6d.
                                            —*Hayfield.*

1662. Getting and leading rushes for ye
        church against ye Bishopp came -   6s. 0d.
1664. Getting and leading rushes for ye
        churche against ye Bishop came -   1s. 6d.
                                            —*Leek.*"

At Hailsham, in Sussex, charges are made in the Churchwardens' Accounts for strewing the church floor with straw or rushes, according to the season of the year; and in the books of the city of Norwich are entries for pea-straw used for a similar purpose. Up to the passing of the Municipal Reform Act the town clerk used to pay to the subsacrist of the cathedral a guinea a year for strewing the floor of the cathedral with rushes on the Mayor's Day, from the western door to the entrance into the choir. At Hardley, in Norfolk, there are entries in the Churchwardens' Accounts for strewing the church with rushes. They commence in the year 1709, and the last is in 1736. The amount paid was 3s. a year, but in some years it is entered in half-yearly payments. After 1736 there is an annual sum of 3s. for mats.

The charity of our ancestors flowed in any channel which led to the service of the church, and the provision of "strewings" for the church floor was not omitted, either by gift or will. The "Reports of the Charity Commissioners" afford several instances.

The Corporation of Bristol pay at Whitsuntide " for ringing and strewing rushes in the church, 3s. 4d. The mayor and a part of the corporation go to Redcliffe church on Whitsunday, when the church is strewed with rushes."—"Charity Reports," viii., p. 607.

At Clee, Lincolnshire, the "parish possesses a right of cutting rushes from a piece of land, the property of Richard Thorold, Esq., called 'Besears,' for the purpose of strewing the floor of the church every Trinity Sunday. A small quantity of grass is annually cut to preserve the right."—"Ibid," xxxii., pt. iv., p. 422.

At Deptford, Kent, "The table of benefactions states that a person unknown gave half a quarter of wheat, to be given in bread every Good Friday, and half a load of rushes at Whitsuntide, and a load of pea-straw at Christmas yearly, for the use of the church. By a decree of the Commissioners for Charitable Uses, dated 4th March, 6 James I. (1609), it was ordered that the owners of three parts of land, whereof one was called Lady Crofts, should from thenceforth for ever deliver and distribute, every Good Friday, amongst the poor people of Deptford, all the bread which might be made and baked of half a quarter of good wheat; and should likewise yearly deliver at Whitsuntide half a load of good green rushes, and at Christmas one good load of new grass straw, in the pews of the church at Deptford. The land charged is Brookley farm. By an order of the vestry, 17 April, 1721, it appears that William Wilkinson offered 21s. per annum for the time to come, in lieu of pea-straw and rushes, which offer was accepted, and since the year 1744, 10s. has been received in lieu of the half quarter of wheat. The two sums of 21s. and 10s. are regularly paid, and distributed in bread."—"Ibid," xxx., p. 618.

At Wingrave, Bucks, "there is a piece of land, of about three roods of meadow, left for the purpose of furnishing rushes for the church on the feast Sunday. It is let to Mr. Thomas Cook, at a rent of 21s. a year, which is received by the parish clerk, who provides grass to strew the church, on the village feast day, which is the first Sunday after St. Peter's day (29 June)."—"Ibid," xxvii., p. 108.

At Glenfield, Leicestershire, "A close, called the Church Acre, was set out, on the inclosure of Glenfield, in lieu of lands in the open fields, the rent of which has always been paid to the clerk of the parish, as a part of his salary. The land is situated near the village, and is let to Joseph Ellis for 30s. a year. In respect of this land the clerk is obliged to strew the church with new hay on the first Sunday after the 5th of July, and for this purpose he is allowed to take a cut of hay from off the land. This practice is understood to be in compliance with the will of the donor of the land."—"Ibid," xxxii., pt. x., p. 158.

At Old Weston, Huntingdonshire, "A piece of green sward, of about a rood, in the open field, belongs by custom to the parish clerk for the time being, subject to the condition of the land being mown immediately before Weston feast, which occurs in July, and the cutting thereof being strewed on the church floor, previously to divine service on the feast Sunday, and continuing there during divine service."—"Ibid," xxiv., p. 57. In August, 1886, the nave and aisle of the church were covered on the feast day with grass cut the previous day on the land bequeathed for that purpose. This is said to be in accordance with a bequest left by an old lady who disliked the noise of the rusties' boots in coming into church.

Collinson, in his "History and Antiquities of the County of Somerset,"* speaking of Tatton, says that "John Lane, of this parish, gent., left half an acre of ground, called the Groves, to the poor for ever, reserving a quantity of the grass for strewing the church on Whitsunday."

* 1791, vol. 3, p. 620.

Rudder * also says that at South Cerney "was a custom, which prevailed till lately, of strewing coarse hay and rushes over the floor of the church, which is called 'Juncare,' and the lands which were subject to provide these materials now pay a certain sum of money annually in lieu thereof."

Redcliffe Church, Bristol, is still adorned with flowers and strewed with rushes on Whitsunday, in accordance with the will of William Mede, who gave a tenement in 1494 to defray the expense, and for a sermon, etc. †

Of the parish of Middleton Chenduit, in Northamptonshire, Bridges ‡ writes : " It is a custom here to strew the Church in summer with Hay gathered from six or seven swaths in Ashmeadow, which have been given for this purpose. The rector finds straw in winter."

* "History of Gloucestershire," 1779, p. 328.
† Taylor's "Bristol," p. 165.
‡ "History of Northamptonshire."

Carrying Rushes to Church.

ORIGINALLY it seems to have been the practice for the parishioners to carry the rushes to church in bundles. As the custom became more of a festival, these were ornamented, and were then borne by young men and maidens dressed in their best attire, and bearing flowers to decorate the church. This method prevailed all over the country, but in South-East Lancashire a far more elaborate arrangement grew up. The rushes, which at one time had been brought to church on sledges, formed into the shape of a haystack, were placed in a cart, and the ingenuity of the people soon made this into an exceedingly novel and pleasing spectacle. Village vied with village in the beauty and size of their rush-carts; rivalry led to expensive ornaments; music and morris dancers followed, till the rush-bearing became a pageant, which once seen is rarely forgotten. Though common objects at the wakes till about twenty years since, they are now rare, and a few more years will probably see the last. One cause is the going away from home to the seaside of the people at the wakes, leaving their own festival to take care of itself. The difficulty of obtaining rushes, owing to the draining of the land, in sufficiently large quantities to fill a cart, still less a waggon as of olden time, has, in many places, led to the abandonment of the custom. Few men are now to be found who are able to build a rush-cart, or who have seen one built; and the labour required also is often considered too much to be given for nothing.

Many learned persons have attempted to trace the origin of a very simple and easily-explained custom in the mists of antiquity, and have attributed mystic meanings to it, which, however, appear to exist only in their own imagination. "A simple observation of the Suio-Gothic etymologist, Ihre, on the Scandinavian *Julhalm*, or straw of Yule, dissipates the learned conjectures of antiquaries as to the origin of the custom of strewing floors with straw and rushes. . . Rudbeck, according to Ihre, derives the Julhalm from the rites of Ceres, while others suppose it to be a commemoration of the Virgin and Child in the stable, but Ihre more reasonably ascribes it to a natural desire to keep the feet warm, although, as he says, the custom was not peculiar to the northern climates, since it was also observed at festivals in France." *

Glover † says the custom was "undoubtedly a relic of Druidism, as on the days of sacrifice we find that the places consecrated to the worship of the ancient British deities were strewn with rushes;" but Hampson (p. 343) more justly observes : "In the feast of the dedication of the church, nothing seems more likely than that the people should supply the building with new rushes, and the ceremony of carrying them in procession on that day merely made a part of the ordinary festivities."

In 1842, Mr. George Shaw, of Saddleworth, wrote to some of the leading antiquaries in the country, describing the custom, and asking their opinion as to its origin. The following extract from a letter by Sir Samuel Rush Meyrick, is dated at Goodrich Court, 7th February, 1842 :

"A thousand thanks for your clear and satisfactory representation and account of the curious custom of Rush-bearing. But in an

---

* Hampson's "Medii Ævi Kalendarium," 1841, vol. 1, p. 340.
† "History of Derbyshire," 1829, vol. 1, p. 305.

RUSH-BEARING.

appeal to me you depend on a Rush, for I cannot help you to any information respecting my namesake. I know of nothing in the practices of the Pagan Britons or Saxons, nor in their religious ceremonies, that has the least reference to its origin. Indeed, as strewing the ground or floors with such materials in Temples which have no other canopy but the sky would have been a needless waste of labour, we cannot look further back than the Introduction of Christianity, nor with any certainty before that was established as the National worship. This brings us to the latter end of the 3d and commencement of the 4th Century. With respect to a shrine being the model, I can say nothing in corroboration. The *delutora* of the ancients were in the form of a boat, or an ordinary chest, as the Ark of the Covenant. Of the boat-shape, or resemblance to a sheer truck, we may still find traces in the Pelew Islands, New Zealand, and other places in the South Seas. Now I myself have never seen any Roman Catholic Shrines but what resemble the Nave of a Church with its high pitched roof, from the Anglo-Saxon time to that of the Fifteenth Century. I can easily imagine the Romish Clergy impressing on their flocks that it was a meritorious act to supply rushes, and that this, by degrees, created a rivalry, which, heightened by the chivalrous feeling exerted from the willing aid of tasteful or anxious sweethearts, would lead to great embellishment. The convex conical form, it appears to me, would be suggested, *ex necessitate rei*, as the sledge could hold but little unless the load were filled up in that manner, and then long twigs (now succeeded by iron rods) at the angles would be requisite to keep it from falling. Narrow gaps and confined roads would prevent any idea of extending the burden laterally. As to the Royal Arms, they would not be a decoration before the period of the Reformation, previous to which, as each Rush-bearing was designed for the Church, it might have displayed the sign of the Cross.

" . . . The Puritan Magistrates and Ministers were opposed to the ancient custom of bearing the Rushes to the Churches, probably from the intemperance and indecorum which generally attended the ceremony. In the Declaration which James 1st put forth in the 15th year of his reign, whilst in Lancashire, it was ordered 'that *Women* should have leave to carry *Rushes* to the Church, for the Decoring of it according to their old custom.'* This was revived injudiciously by Ch. 1., in 1635."

James I. no doubt made the Declaration referred to through the representations of the people of Lancashire when he visited the county in 1617. The desired license was granted to the people of Lancashire only.

* Fuller's "Church History," 6, x, p. 24.

but its extension to the whole of England, by the publication of the "Book of Sports," on the 24th May, 1618, from the Manor of Greenwich, was occasioned by a misuse of his informal assent to the petition. During his stay at Hoghton Tower he witnessed many Lancashire amusements, amongst them a "rush-bearing," on the 17th July.

In "Whimzies, or, a New Cast of Characters," 1631, 12mo, a zealous brother, it is said, "denounceth a heavie woe upon all Wakes, Summerings, and *Rush-bearings*, preferring that an act whereby pipers were made rogues, by Act of Parliament, before any in all the *Acts and Monuments;*" and of a pedlar the author says: "A Country Rush-bearing, or Morrice-Pastoral, is his Festivall: if ever he aspire to plum-porridge, that is the day. Here the guga-girles gingle it with his neat nifles."

So also, in Brathwaite's "Ar't Asleepe Husband?: A Boulster Lecture" (1640) we find: "Such an one as not a Rush-bearer or May-morrish in all that Parish could subsist without him."

A passage in a satirical work of the seventeenth century (Clitus's "Whimzies," p. 132), speaking of a country braggadocio, says: "His sovereignty is showne highest at May games, wakes, summerings, and *rush-bearings;* where it is twentie to one but hee becomes beneficial to the lord of the mannoure by meanes of a bloody nose or a broken pate,"—that is, fined for breaking the peace.

At Donnington, in Lincolnshire, the ancient custom of strewing church floors with rushes was some time ago annually observed on St. Bartholomew's Day (25th August). In the morning a number of maidens, clad in their best attire, went in procession to a small chapel then standing in the parish, and strewed the floor with rushes; they next proceeded to a piece of land known as the "Play Garths," where they were met by the inhabitants, and the remainder of the day was spent in rustic games.*

The custom of carrying bundles of rushes to decorate the church is yet observed at Ambleside, Borrowdale, and Grasmere, in the Lake District. By the kindness of the late Llewellyn Jewitt, Esq., I am enabled to give the plate of the Rush-bearing at Borrowdale, from the "Life and Works of Jacob Thompson,"† together with the following description of it. The picture is the property of Richard Radcliffe, Esq., of Byrkley Lodge.

"The companion picture [to the 'Vintage'] the 'Rush-bearing,' is as thoroughly illustrative of North of England scenery as 'The Vintage' is of that of Northern Italy, and in conception, grouping, and treatment the two will vie with each other in artistic excellence. As a study of mountainous scenery in one of the most romantic and beautiful districts of English lakeland, it is 'without fault or blemish;' and if the artist's imaginative mind and poetic temperament *have* run wild in giving to the procession of rush-bearers a character and an extent not their own, he has, by so doing, produced a picture pre-eminently lovely, and more than pleasing to the eye. The subject, of course, is the old rural custom of 'rush-bearing,' *i.e.*, the bringing home of the last load of rushes— literally the 'harvest home' of rush-gathering— for the strewing of the floors of church and homestead. The custom, formerly pretty general, and held to with tenacity in the mountainous districts of Westmoreland and the High Peak of Derbyshire, has now become all but obsolete. In one district with which I am acquainted the rushes, gathered and tied up in small sheaves, ornamented with ribbons, coloured papers, and sometimes improvised masks, were piled up, in form of a pyramid, in a cart or waggon, and the whole decorated with wreaths of flowers or 'greens,' and surmounted by a garland or flag. Drawn by men or horses, also liberally ornamented with ribbons and flowers, the load of rushes was taken through the village, preceded by a band of music, and accompanied by a crowd of people to the church gates, where it was unloaded, the 'decking' taken off, and the rushes carried into the building and strewed on the floor, both in and out of the pews, the garlands being hung up near the chancel. The custom seems to have been pretty much the same in the Westmoreland villages, and Mr. Thompson has 'poeticised' it by seating a 'queen' on the car, surrounded by garland-bearing maidens.

"The landscape is that of Borrowdale, the charming and eminently

---

* "History of the County of Lincoln," 1834, vol. 2, p. 255.
† 1882, pp. 78-81.

RUSH-BEARING, FROM THE ORIGINAL PAINTING BY JACOB THOMPSON.

Reprinted, by permission, from "THE LIFE AND WORKS OF JACOB THOMPSON," by Llewellynn Jewitt, F.S.A.

picturesque little village of Borrowdale Grange, with its whitewashed cottages and rural bridge, being beautifully rendered to the right, and the grand mountain range rising up, cloud-capped to the skies. From this village the procession, numbering some sixty or more figures, is supposed to have started, and to be wending its way up the hill, and round a lovely wooded knoll covered with herbage, to the church on the left, near which are depicted, in all their sombre tint, the yew-trees immortalised by Wordsworth as the

> '. . . Fraternal Four of Borrowdale,
> Joined in one solemn and capacious grove;
> Huge trunks! and each particular trunk a growth
> Of intertwisted fibres, serpentine,
> Up coiling, and inveterately convolved.'

The church among the trees on the knoll, I ought to add, is in reality that of Morland, which, from its picturesque character, just accorded with the painter's views, and was accordingly introduced. Among the figures are many portraits of well-known people—among the rest, Mrs. Lowther, wife of Capt. F. W. Lowther, who sat for the 'Queen' in the procession: the late Rev. Dr. Jackson, Provost of Queen's College, Oxford, and his then curate, but now successor in the rectory of Lowther, the Rev. T. B. Tylecote; and several of the villagers; and it is interesting to add that the picture was, in the main, painted at one of the houses, that of Mr. Threlkeld, in the village of Borrowdale Grange, represented in the composition. . .

"As previously with the 'Vintage,' so with the 'Rush-bearing,' this magnificent picture, on its completion, called forth many expressions of profound admiration, both in prose and verse, from the few who had the good fortune to be permitted to see it. Among these the following lines, addressed to the painter by the Rev. James Dixon, are eminently worth here printing:

> 'Fresh from the blazing orient o'er the sea,
> The morning with its golden wings alights
> On mountain tops, that lift their granite walls
> Against the dark grey of the western sky.
> The shadows in the valleys far below
> Vanish, and leave all here in morning light—
> The farmstead gleaming through its sycamores,
> And village by the bridge, a woody cliff,
> And mead with groups of cattle in its lap,
> And pale stream that keeps wakeful all the night,
> Nor ever stays its silvery foot to rest;
> And glassy level of the silent mere,
> Within whose deep the mountain's golden crown,
> And all the panorama of the rocks
> And star-travelled regions of the sky, behold
> Their counterfeit magnificent.

'It is so calm,
So fair, so sweet, such brilliancy of colour,
Such fresh and dewy atmosphere, that I
Could wish the morning for awhile would stay
Its flight on yon high mountain. 'Tis a present
No past can dim, no future can outshine,
Such as shall hang on memory's pictured walls
For future contemplation, when the din
And fretful stir of daily life has fallen,
And in the silence of our souls we hear
The low sweet voices of departed days.

The dalesmen are astir betimes in summer,
When dewy fields, knee-deep with grass and flowers,
Await the cutting. Columns of blue smoke
Rise from the village: in a neighbouring mead,
That skirts the mere, a mower whets his scythe,
And echo blows her silver horn on high
From the hoar summit of a channelled cliff;
The milkmaid sings a love song as she goes
Down the green lane, festooned with eglantine,
To milk her cows, that low at her approach;
And children are come forth to greet the morn
With the bright welcome of their rosy smiles.

But there is stir unwonted, for to-day
The valley keeps an ancient festival;
And by the sun has clomb the morning sky
Above the purple ridges of the east
All toil is over. Here and there are seen
Gay groups of country folk in Sunday suit,
With mirth and joyance winding through the vale,
Down mountain passes from the neighbouring dales,
And by the gleaming margin of the lake,
And some in boats with banners on its breast.
A flag droops idly on the grey church tower,
When forth the bells clash out their jubilee,
And fling their ancient music through the air:
Round after round from brazen throat leaps out,
Till all the rocks reverberate: far away
On yon blue mountain breast the softened sounds
Hang like enchantment; there is not a heart
But beats with sober gladness; even they
Who waste with sickness, or are bowed with grief,
Forget their sorrows in the common joy.

And now the grand procession is arranged,
And through the village moves toward the church,

'The old and young, the rich and poor, are met,
Sharing one common happiness alike;
The old with thoughts that slip back on the past,
The young with fancies bright as their own smiles,
Painting the sunny future of their lives.
Conspicuous in the van, on the hill's slope,
The parish priest ascends, a grey-haired man,
Of aspect venerable and stature tall,
Of reputation such as a whole life
Spent in well-doing could alone achieve.
High honours in the schools had crowned his youth,
High dignities in the church his riper years;
But dearer far to him of all his honours,
And most esteemed, is that of parish priest,
The sacred functions of whose holy office
Now for a generation he has filled.
Following, the lord and lady from the hall
Do honour to the time-worn festival,
Stepping from their exalted rank awhile
To walk on even terms with peasant life,
And by sublime democracy attest
The common heirs we all are of the past,
The common bonds that bind us in the present,
The common hopes that with mild splendour light
The life, the death, the life again, for all.
But priest and squire, grey rock and glassy lake,
And village dreaming of its own white walls,
And all the pictured mystery of the hills—
These all are but the setting to one group,
Which, in the foreground, 'neath the sycamore,
That spreads its emerald umbrage to the sky,
Moves with a motion every line displays,
And floods the space with beauty like a gleam
Of golden sunshine shot from a riven cloud
Upon the unsunned scenery of a vale:
There in the midst, throned on a rustic sledge
Frilled high with rushes in their greenness gathered,
The queen of beauty sits, in youthful bloom
The frost of Time's fierce winter shall not nip,
And round her hang a garland of fair maids,
Fair as herself, with wreaths of flowers yoked
In deathless fellowship of fairest fame.
Moving to the music of their own rich charms
In mystic dance of grace that fascinates
And keeps the head in thraldom while we gaze
And memory lasts.

> 'And still the bells ring out,
> Making melodious chimings in the air;
> And still the living group moves up the hill,
> And all the glory of that summer day
> In its serenity of loveliness abides;
> No cloud to gloom the freshness of its colours,
> No night to fall upon it from the sky,
> And blot it out for ever. As we gaze,
> Our souls are all suffused with what we see—
> The comeliness of old religious ways
> That sanctify the current of our life,
> Blended with one of nature's matchless moods,
> Caught by the genius of the artist's hand,
> To enrich the generations yet to come
> In grand succession, until day and night
> Shall fold their wings on the everlasting shore.'"

A description of the rush-bearing at Ambleside, in 1885, was given in the "Queen,"* it says:

"As the town clock chimes 6 p.m. a band is heard in the distance, and soon there comes down the main street of the town a procession of young children —boys and girls— carrying devices of wooden framework, covered with rushes, moss, and flowers. Leading the procession is a sweet-faced country lassie of eleven or twelve years of age, carrying the churchwardens' rush-bearing, a plain upright piece of wood, covered entirely with the green rushes gathered from the lake ; then follows a bonnie blue-eyed boy bearing a device in the shape of a harp, whose strings are formed of white peeled rushes, with the boards or frame thickly adorned with the white water lilies. Crosses of all kinds hung on moss-clad staffs, every shape and device which the ingenuity and taste of the ladies of the parish could design, and which the richness or delicacy of greenhouse exotics or the native flowers of the field could adorn, appear, borne by the long line of school-children who form the procession. When at length the garlands have all been brought into the market-place, a halt is made, the 'rush-bearings' are all placed in the street, and a gay scene it is which the town for the next ten minutes presents. . . . But the children are taking up their crosses, the band commences the first bars of a march, and the procession begins to move onwards towards the church. When the churchyard is reached the children carry their floral offerings into the sacred edifice, and the doors are locked to all others for a short time, whilst the garlands are deposited in the chancel aisle and windows. This done, the congregation is admitted into the church, and join in a short service, consisting of prayer, hymn, and a

---

* See "Public Opinion," 2nd October, 1885, p. 425.

brief address. The hymn which is sung is known as 'The Rush-bearing Hymn,'* and, as descriptive of the origin, as well as the reason for the commemoration of the custom which is being celebrated, is worth quoting :

'Our fathers to the house of God,
  As yet a building rude,
Bore offerings from the flowery sod,
  And fragrant rushes strewed.

May we, their children, ne'er forget
  The pious lesson given,
But honour still, together met,
  The Lord of earth and heaven.

Sing we the great Creator's praise,
  Who sends us sun and showers,
To cheer our hearts with fruitful days,
  And deck our world with flowers.

These of the great Redeemer's grace
  Bright emblems here are seen !
He makes to smile the desert place
  With flowers and rushes green !'

The rush-bearings remain in the church over the Sunday until the following Monday afternoon, when the children again meet and bear them through the town to a field, where an ordinary school treat is given, and so ends the Rush-bearing Festival of that particular year."

" . . . At Grasmere, the Rush-bearing Festival was commemorated this year three weeks later in the season than usual. The patron saint of the ancient Grasmere church is Oswald, and the vicar of the parish, after consulting the desires of his parishioners, this year determined upon St. Oswald's Day [5th August] for the Rush-bearing Festival. In almost every respect the festival is observed here in the same manner as at Ambleside ; but the church, being situate in the very centre of the village, the custom at Grasmere is for the children to meet together in the churchyard, and place their rush-bearings on the wall of the churchyard, where they remain for about half-an-hour, to be inspected by the crowd of people who are collected there."

The annexed engraving represents the rush-bearing at Grasmere in 1888, from a sketch by Miss Wintle, in the " Graphic," 22nd June, 1889 (pp. 676, 682). The " rush-bearings " are generally tall crosses or shepherds'

---

* Composed by the Rev. Owen Lloyd, an accomplished young clergyman, curate of Ambleside, who died, much lamented, about 1838 or 1840.

crooks. The design is made in rushes, and stands from one to four feet high, the whole is ornamented, often covered with flowers, and in some cases the result is very beautiful. They are placed on boards along the edge of the pews.

A correspondent, "T.Q.M.," writing to Hone's "Year Book," (pp. 553-4) 21st July, 1827, describes the custom as then practised at Grasmere:—

"The church door was open, and I discovered that the villagers were strewing the floors with fresh rushes. I learnt from the old clerk, that, according to annual custom, the rush-bearing procession would be in the evening. . . During the whole of this day I observed the children busily employed in preparing garlands of such wild flowers as the beautiful valley produces, for the evening procession, which commenced at nine, in the following order: The children (chiefly girls), holding these garlands, paraded through the village, preceded by the *Union* band (thanks to the great drum for this information), they then entered the church, where the three largest garlands were placed on the altar, and the remaining ones in various other parts of the place. . . In the procession I observed the 'Opium Eater' [De Quincey], Mr. Barber, an opulent gentleman residing in the neighbourhood, Mr. and Mrs. Wordsworth, Miss Wordsworth, and Miss Dora Wordsworth. Wordsworth is the chief supporter of these rustic ceremonies. The procession over, the party adjourned to the ball-room, a hayloft, at my worthy friend Mr. Bell's, where the country lads and lasses tripped it merrily and *heavily*.

. . . The rush-bearing is now, I believe, almost entirely confined to Westmoreland. It was once customary in Craven, as appears from the following extract from Dr. Whittaker:—

'Among the seasons of periodical festivity was the rush-bearing, or the ceremony of conveying fresh rushes to strew the floor of the parish church. This method of covering floors was universal in *houses* while floors were of earth, but is now confined to places of worship; the bundles of the girls were adorned with wreaths of flowers, and *the evening concluded with a dance*. In Craven the custom has wholly ceased.'

In Westmoreland, the custom has undergone a change. Billy [Dawson, the fiddler, who had been the officiating minstrel for the last six-and-forty years], remembered when the lasses bore the rushes in the evening procession, and strewed the church floor at the same time that they decorated the church with garlands; now, the rushes are laid in the morning by the ringer and clerk, and no rushes are introduced in the evening procession. I do not like old customs to change, for, like mortals, they change before they die altogether."

At Marton, a small village on the shores of Morecambe Bay, the rush-bearing was observed on the dedication-day, 5th August, the patron saint being St. Oswald, or on the Sunday nearest St. Oswald's. Lucas, a schoolmaster here, wrote a history of the neighbourhood, still in manuscript,* and, referring to the customs of the district, observes that:

"The vain custom of dancing, excessive drinking, etc., having been many years laid aside, the inhabitants and strangers spend that day in duly attending the service of the church, and making good cheer, within the rules of sobriety, in private houses; and the next in several kinds of diversions, the chiefest of which is usually a rush-bearing, which is in this manner. They cut hard rushes from the marsh, which they make up into long bundles, and then dress them in fine linen, silk ribands, flowers, etc.; afterwards the young women of the village, which perform the ceremony that year, take up the burdens erect, and begin the procession (precedence being always given to the churchwardens' burden), which is attended not only with multitudes of people, but with music, drums, ringing of bells, and all other demonstrations of joy they are able to express. When they arrive at the church, they go in at the west end (the only public use that I ever saw that door put to), and setting down their burdens in the church, strip them of their ornaments, leaving the heads or crowns of them decked with flowers, cut paper, etc., in some part of the church, generally over the cancelli. Then the company return to the town, and cheerfully partake of a plentiful collation provided for that purpose, and spend the remaining part of the day, and frequently a great part of the night also, in dancing, if the weather permits, about a may-pole adorned with greens and flowers, or else in some other convenient place."

* There is a copy of this MS. in the Watson MSS., Bodelian Library, Oxford, vol. 4, folio.

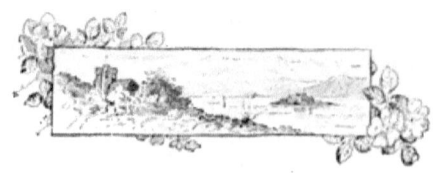

The Rush-Cart.

SOUTH-EAST Lancashire was the home of the rush-cart. Almost every village had one, and the rivalry between the people sometimes rose to such a pitch that bloodshed occurred. Our information, therefore, is more complete and varied here that can be obtained elsewhere. Many writers have alluded to the custom, and given illustrations of the rush-cart; painters, too, have depicted the scene; and poets gone into raptures over it.* Elijah Ridings, a Lancashire poet, in his "Village Festival,"† writes :

> "Behold the rush-cart and the throng
> Of lads and lasses pass along !
> Now watch the nimble morris-dancers,
> Those blithe, fantastic, antic prancers,
> Bedecked with gaudiest profusion
> Of ribbons in a gay confusion
> Of brilliant colours, richest dyes,
> Like wings of moths and butterflies ;
> Waving white kerchiefs here and there,
> And up and down and everywhere.
> Springing, bounding, gaily skipping,
> Deftly, briskly, no one tripping.
> All young fellows, blithe and hearty,
> Thirty couples in the party ;
> And on the footpaths may be seen
> Their sweethearts from each lane and green
> And cottage home ; all fain to see
> This festival of rural glee ;

* There is said to be a little pamphlet entitled "The Rush-bearing : A Poem," printed at Huddersfield in 1784, but I have been unable to meet with a copy.
† "Village Muse," 1854, pp. 28-29.

> "The love betrothed, the fond heart plighted,
> And with the witching scene delighted;
> In modest guise and simple graces,
> With roses blushing on their faces.
> Behold the strong-limbed horses stand,
> The pride and boast of English land,
> Fitted to move in shafts or chains,
> With plaited glossy tails and manes;
> Their proud heads each a garland wears
> Of quaint devices—suns and stars,
> And roses, ribbon-wrought, abound;
> The silver plate, one hundred pounds.
> With green oak boughs the cart is crowned,
> The strong, gaunt horses shake the ground."

Roby,* writing in 1829, speaks of the custom as

"An unmeaning pageant still practised in the northern and eastern parts of Lancashire, for the purpose of levying contributions on the inhabitants. An immense banner of silk, adorned with tinsel and gay devices, precedes the rush-cart, wherein the rushes, neatly woven and smoothly cut, are piled up, and decorated with flowers and ribands, in rustic taste. The cart, thus laden, is drawn round to the dwellings of the principal inhabitants by morris-dancers, who perform an uncouth dance, attended by a man in motley attire, a sort of nondescript, made up of the ancient fool and Maid Marian. This personage jingles a horse-collar hung with bells, which forms not an unsuitable accompaniment to the ceremony."

Roby's description is so brief and inaccurate that we turn to Harland and Wilkinson's "Lancashire Legends," † for information as to rush-bearing in East Lancashire. They say:

"These used to have a real significance. The rushes were cut, dried, and then carried in carts to the churchyard. The rushes were then strewn along the aisles of the church and in the bottoms of the pews, in preparation for winter. Carpets and cushions (locally termed 'wishons,') were then unknown, except in the pews of the wealthy. Barrowford rush-bearing is always held on the first Sunday after the 19th August. This festival is still visited by vast numbers of persons from Burnley, Colne, Padiham, and elsewhere. Cheap trips are run on the East Lancashire line from Burnley and Colne to Nelson Station. Riot and drunkenness reign supreme. Rush-bearing

---

* "Traditions of Lancashire," 5th edition, 1872, note p. 264.
† 1873, pp. 111-112.

THE BY-STANDERS.

Sundays are also observed at other places, as Holme, Worsthorn, Downham, etc., but usually not in so disreputable a manner. Most of the clergy take advantage of those Sundays, and fix their 'charity sermons' for those days. They thus obtain contributions from many distant friends, who pay special visits to their relatives on these occasions. In Yorkshire these pastimes take the name of 'feasts.'"

We have, however, to turn to Bamford's "Early Days,"[*] for a complete account of the rush-cart, and the manner in which it was made:

"But 'The Rush-bearing' was the great feast of the year, and was held on the anniversary of the dedication of the church. At Middleton it is held on the third Saturday in August, or, if there be five Saturdays in the month, it falls on the fourth. From tradition, as well as from the custom itself, we may conclude that at first it was a simple offering towards making the church floor comfortable during the winter services. Every family having then its separate bench to sit upon, some one or two of them would at first strew their own floors with rushes to promote the warmth of their feet during the stormy months. Others, perceiving how snugly and cosily their neighbours sat, would follow the example. Probably the priest would encourage the new luxury, and it would soon become common. Thus Nan and Dick, and Bob and Bet, would be seen carrying bundles of rushes to the church at the feast of the dedication, and the church would be littered for the winter. Next, families forming small hamlets of the parish would unite, and, pitching each their quota of rushes into a cart, would send down their load. Some of these hamlets, in order probably to ingratiate themselves with the priest by rendering extra homage to the church, would arrange and decorate their rushes with green boughs; others would excel them; and a rivalry as to which hamlet could bring the neatest formed and most finely decorated load of rushes would ensue; and thus the present quaint and graceful 'rush-cart' would be in time produced. Music, dancing, and personal finery would accompany and keep pace with the increasing display; the feast would become a spectacle for all the surrounding districts, and the little wood-shaded village would annually become a scene of a joyous gathering and a hospitable festivity, and thus the wakes, as they existed in my early days, would be gradually produced.

"The folds or hamlets which mostly sent rush-carts to Middleton, were Boarshaw, Thornham, Hopwood, Birch, Bowlee, and Tonge. About a month or six weeks before the wakes, the young men of the hamlets, as well as those of the town, would meet at their

* 1849, pp. 146-154.

respective rendezvous, which was some ale-house, where the names of such as wished to join the party during the wakes were given in, and the first instalment of money was paid. These meetings were called 'enterings,' and they always took place on Sunday evenings, when each one paid a certain sum towards a general fund, and a trifle more for drink at their meetings. It was the interest of these young fellows to raise as strong a party as they could, not only with a view to a plenteous fund, but also in order to repel, if necessary, aggression from other parties, for, as these little communities were seldom without a few old grudges to fall back upon should an opportunity offer, it was very extraordinary indeed if a quarrel did not take place amongst some of them, and half-a-dozen battles were not foughten, before the wakes ended. It was consequently an object with each to get as numerous a party, and as heavily-bodied an one, as they could, agility and science not being so requisite in Lancashire battles as weight, strength, and endurance. These young fellows therefore mustered as imposingly as they could, and if one or two of the young women of the place happened to have sweethearts who came from a distance—and especially if they were likely to clear their way in a row—the courters would probably be found joined with the brothers and friends of their fair ones. Well, the 'enterings' having been formed, and the subscriptions duly paid, a rush-cart would be determined upon. Such a farmer's broad-wheeled cart was to be bespoke. Then lads and lasses would, at all spare hours, be engaged in some preparation for the feast. New clothes would be ordered, and their quantity and quality would probably depend on the amount of money saved during the year, or on the work performed in a certain time before the wakes. Jack would obtain, if he could, a 'bran new suit, wi' trindl't shirt;' and Bess would have her 'geawn made wi' tucks an' fleawnees; new shoon wi' ston op heels; new stockins wi' clocks; a tippit wi' frills all reawnd, monny a streng o' necklaces; an' a bonnit made by th' new mantymaker, the prattyist 'at ever wur seen, wi' a skyey blue underside, an' pink ribbins.' By 'day-strike' in a morning, or by 'neet-gloom' in the evening, the jingle of morrice-bells would be heard along the lanes and field-roads, for the lads, having borrowed each his collar of bells at neighbouring farmhouses, would hang them on their necks and come jingling them home, waking all the echoes in the deep lanes, and the meadow-nooks, and the old grey solitary places, until the very air was clamourous of the bell tingle and the musical roll of the crotal. Ropes and stretchers would also be borrowed, and the rushes growing in certain waste pieces having been marked out, and, when necessary, bargained for with the owner of the land, mowers were appointed, and a day or two before the commencement of the wakes the rushes were cut down. An old experienced hand was generally engaged to 'make the cart,' that is, to lay on, and build up, and trim the rushes, according to the design which is always adopted in such constructions. The girls meanwhile would all be employed at over-hours getting their own finery and that of their brothers or sweethearts ready for the great event. Tinsel was purchased; hats were trimmed with ribbons and fanciful devices; shirts were washed, bleached snow-white, and neatly plated; tassels, and garlands, and wreaths of coloured paper, tinsel, and ribbon, were designed and constructed, and a grand piece of ingenuity and splendour, a kind of concentration of the riches and the pomp of the party was displayed in the arrangements and setting forth of 'the sheet.' This was exclusively the work of the girls and women; and, in proportion, as it was happily designed and fitly put together, or otherwise, was their praise or disparagement meted out by the public, a point on which they would probably be not a little sensitive. The sheet was a piece of very white linen, generally a good bed-sheet, and on it were arranged pretty rosettes, and quaint compartments and borderings of all colours and hues which either paper, tinsel, or ribbons, or natural flowers could supply. In these compartments were arrayed silver watches, trays, spoons, sugar-tongs, teapots, snuffers, or other fitting articles of ornament and value, and the more numerous and precious the articles were, the greater was the deference which the party which displayed them expected from the wondering crowd. Musicians were also secured in good time; a fiddler for the chamber-dancing always, and never less than a couple of fifers and a drummer to play before the cart. But if the funds would allow, and especially in later times, a band of instrumentalists would be engaged, often a sorry affair certainly, but still 'a band' to swear to, and that would be a great thing for the ears of the multitude. All true churchgoers were duly apprised of the wakes, as its date was cried by the bell-man in the churchyard whilst the congregation were leaving the church, on three Sunday afternoons previous to its commencement. The morning of the great day comes, and everyone is in a state of bustle and anxiety. Heads of families are bundling up their work and hastening off to town in order to be back in time for the opening of the wakes. And now, the rushes having been mown, are carted to the place where the cart is to be made. The maker, with his assistants, are all present; the wheels are sunken in holes, and the cart is well-propped to make it steady; the peeled rods and binders are set up so as to make the structure steady, and to give the proper form as it advances; ale is poured out and drunk liberally; numerous youngsters are playing and rolling about on the rush-heap, whilst others are making of them small sheaves, bound at each end, and, being cut in the middle with a scythe-blade, are called 'bowls' (bolts); others again are culling the finest of the rushes, and making them into 'bowls' of a superior description wherewith to form a neat edging to the front and back of the structure. And so they keep binding, and cutting, and piling up until 'the cart' is completed, which now presents the form almost of a flattened bee-hive, with the ends also flattened and ornamented with a projecting edging of rush-bolts, which gives them a quaint and trim appearance. The sheet before described is displayed with all its wonder-exciting treasures in front of the cart, sometimes another sheet, less costly, is exhibited behind, and when that is not the case, letters and various devices in flowers are generally found there. The top of the cart, or rush-heap, is stuck with green boughs, which wave and nod like plumes, and amongst them one or two of the young men, who have been the latest married, take their seats astride the load. The drawers, all don'd in ribbon, finery, and tinsel, now begin to make their appearance, some dozen or so of the leaders having bells around their necks. The drum is beating, the music is blowing and snorting and screaming, the gay tinkle of morrice-bells is floating and waking up the echoes. The children are wild with joyful expectation, or astonished by the wonderous fairy scene. The girls, bepranked in their new pumps, kirtles, and bonnets, now add beauty to the spectacle; and on the arm of each may be noticed the best Sunday coat and doublet of her brother or her sweetheart. The ropes are attached; the stretchers noosed fast at proper distances; all is ready. The music strikes up louder; the driver clears the way with his long-whip, making it give a loud and clear crack at every stroke—that being his feat—the word is 'Neaw lads,' and at one strong pull and a heave of the shafts the wheels are dislodged from their socket-holes, and the cart is slowly drawn up to the level sward, amid the loud shouts of the admiring gazers; and so, with music-clangour, and bell-jingle, and laughter, and words of caution, as 'Howd on, lads,' 'Gently, lads,' the quaint and romantically fantastic spectacle moves towards the village of its destination.

"If the party can go to the expense of having a set of morrice-dancers, and feel inclined to undertake the trouble, some score or two of young men, with hats trimmed, and decked out as before described, precede the drawers, dancing in couples to various simple country tunes, one of which may be measured by this stanza:

'My new shoon they are so good,
  I cou'd doance morris if I wou'd;
An' if hat an' sark be drest,
  I will doance morris wi' the best.'

"In some later instances there have been processions of banner and garland bearers, with all beautiful flowers, artificial or real, and apt and ingenious devices. A choice beauty of the village may also, on some occasions, be induced to personate the Queen of the Wake, walking under a bower borne by four of her companions, and pre-

CARTER AND WHIP.

ceded by dancers and the other pageants described. But these spectacles I should rather suppose to be of comparatively modern introduction in this part of Lancashire.

"Arrived at the village, other parties similar to their own will be found parading their cart on the highroad. The neighbouring folds and hamlets, having been nearly deserted by their inhabitants, all are there concentrated seeing the wakes and partaking in the universal enjoyment. The highway is thronged by visitors in gay attire, whilst shows, nut-stalls, flying-boxes, merry-go-rounds, and other means of amusement are rife on every hand. Should two carts meet, and there be a grudge on either side, a wrangle, and probably a battle or two, settles the question, and they each move on; if the parties are in amity, they salute each other with friendly huzzas, the drawers holding their stretchers above their heads until they have passed. Each cart stops at the door of every public-house, which the leaders enter tumultuously, jumping, jingling their bells, and imitating the neighing of horses. A can of ale is then generally brought to the door and distributed to the drawers and attendants, those who ride on the top not forgetting to claim their share. When the whole town or village has been thus perambulated, the cart is drawn to the green near the church, where the rushes are deposited—or should be —though latterly, since the introduction of pews in the church, they have generally been sold to the best bidder. The moment the first cart arrives on the green, the church bells strike up a merry round peal in honour of those who have thus been alert to testify their devotion; but as the rushes are now seldom left at the church, so neither is the ringing so strictly performed as it was wont to be, and, in fact, though the name and the form are in some degree retained, it is evident that attachment to our venerable state-worship has far less influence in the matter than it had in the days of my early life.

"After disposing of their rushes, either by gift to the church (in which case they became the perquisite of the sexton), or by sale to the best bidder, the lads, and their friends, sweethearts, and helpers, repaired to the public-house at which they put up for the wakes, and there spent the night in drinking and dancing. On Sunday, some of the principal banners and garlands, which had been paraded the day before, were displayed in the church, and on Sunday night the lads and lasses again met at the public-house, where they drank, smoked, and treated their neighbours and friendly visitors from other public-houses."

Of a different character was the rush-bearing described in Miss Louisa Potter's "Lancashire Memories."* Instead of the cart being drawn by a

* 1879, pp. 52-53.

band of young men with ropes and stretchers, horses, gaily decorated, were employed; and this is the more usual custom of late times, though occasionally, where only one horse is used, a number of young men range themselves in front and pull away, but more for display than assistance to the horse. Miss Potter writes:

"In August we had the rush-bearing, which was the annual gathering of rushes to strew the aisles of the parish church, and keep it warm during the winter. The rushes were most artistically piled on a cart, in the form of a haystack: the front was covered with a white cloth, and adorned with silver tankards, cream-jugs, teapots, spoons, arranged in patterns, and whatever could be borrowed in the way of plate, which was always cheerfully lent. These were interspersed with flowers, and always a large G.R. in marigolds, sunflowers, or hollyhocks; dahlias were unknown. The cart was drawn by four, and sometimes six, fine horses, adorned with ribbons, and bells that jingled merrily as they walked. A dozen young men and women, streaming with ribbons, and waving handkerchiefs, preceded the cart, dancing the morris-dance. There was the shepherdess, with a lamb in a basket and a crook in her hand, dressed in white, with a green bower borne over her head, and always two watches at her side. There was the fool, a hideous figure in a horrid mask, with onions for ear-rings and a cow's tail for a pig-tail, belabouring the crowd with an inflated bladder at the end of a very long pole. It was a point of honour to appear much amused with his antics, but many a little heart quaked under its assumed bravery.

"The procession was closed by two garlands, carried aloft, of coloured paper, cut into familiar devices: and, at the close of the day, the rush-cart was taken to pieces, the rushes strewed in the church, and the garlands hung in the chancel, to remain until replaced by new ones the following year."

The following description of the rush-bearing at Heaton, near Manchester, is from Frances Ann Kemble's "Record of a Girlhood" (1878, vol. 2, p. 185), and is contained in a letter sent from Birmingham, 7th September, 1830:

"During the two days, which were all we could spare for Heaton, I walked and rode and sang and talked, and was so well amused and pleased that I hope, after our week's work is over here, we may return there for a short time. I must tell you of a curious little bit of ancientry which I saw at Heaton, which greatly delighted me—a 'rush-bearing.' At a certain period of the year, generally the beginning of autumn, it was formerly the wont in some parts of Lancashire to go round with sundry rustic mummeries to all the churches and strew them with rushes. The religious intention of the custom has passed away, but a pretty rural procession, which I witnessed, still keeps up the memory of it hereabouts. I was sitting at my window, looking out over the lawn, which slopes charmingly on every side down to the house, when the still summer air was suddenly filled with the sound of distant shouts and music, and presently the quaint pageant drew in sight. First came an immense waggon piled with rushes in a stack-like form, on the top of which sat two men holding two huge nosegays. This was drawn by a team of Lord W——'s finest farm-horses, all covered with scarlet cloths, and decked with ribbons and bells and flowers. After this came twelve country lads and lasses, dancing the real old morris-dance, with their handkerchiefs flying, and in all the rustic elegance of apparel which they could command for the occasion. After them followed a very good village band, and then a species of flowery canopy, under which walked a man and woman covered with finery, who, Lord W—— told me, represented Adam and Eve. The procession closed with a fool, fantastically dressed out, and carrying the classical bladder at the end of his stick. They drew up before the house and danced their morris-dance for us. The scraps of old poetry which came into my head, the contrast between this pretty picture of a bygone time and the modern, but by no means unpicturesque, group assembled under the portico, filled my mind with the pleasantest ideas, and I was quite sorry when the rural pageant wound up the woody heights again, and the last shout and peal of music came back across the sunny lawn. I am very glad I saw it."

The author of "Scarsdale" * has given a graphic, but rather exaggerated account of rush-bearings as they were celebrated fifty years ago. He says:

"In front of the inn stood the rush-cart, which, to our southern readers, may require a more detailed description. One of the larger carts, used in Lancashire either to carry manufactured goods or to bring harvest from the field, had been heaped with rushes to the height of about twenty-four feet from the ground. † The rushes were skilfully arranged into a perfectly smooth conical stack, rising to a sharp ridge at the top. From this centre four hedges, formed of rushes woven into a neat pattern, and each hedge about two feet high, descended to the four corners of the cart. On the summit was a bower in the form of a crown, made of holly, laurel, and other ever-

* Sir J. P. Kay-Shuttleworth, 1860, 8vo.
† This is greatly overstated. The carts were usually from ten to twelve feet high, if the latter, it was considered a big one.

greens, round which were twined garlands. An immense wreath of large flowers encircled the base of the arbour, and a smaller one decorated its top. On each of the smooth sides of the cone, between the boundary of rush-hedges, were inscriptions in brilliantly-coloured flowers, such as 'Colliers and Weavers,' 'Fear God,' 'Honour the King,' etc. Spangled flags of various bright hues hung from the sides of the crowning bower. A large silver salver from the Hall, with some silver tankards, hung on the front. About thirty young men, with white shirts down to the waist, profusely adorned with gay ribbons, and with wreaths of flowers on their heads, were yoked in couples between two strong new ropes. Each couple held a stave fastened on either side into a knot in the rope, and they were engaged in practising some dances, with which their entry into the principal streets of Rochdale was to be celebrated. A strong horse was in the shafts, and behind was a band of other gaily-dressed young men, similarly yoked between ropes, to hold the cart while descending any steep hill. A bugle sounded to summon the dancers from the booth, the revellers from the club-room, and the wandering groups and whispering lovers from the garden. Some miles of road had to be traversed, and all the rush-carts from the neighbouring villages were to meet at Rochdale at noon. There issued from behind the house the whole united band, with a big drum, two bugles, two trumpets, several other brass instruments, with fifes, flageolets, etc. They were the heralds of an immense banner, held in the air by four men, two on each side, who grasped long slender poles, supporting a transverse piece, from which swung this mighty achievement of the art of Scarsdale. In the centre were the Scarsdale arms, which had never been so fiercely emblazoned before. On the top was a view of Scarsdale Hall, painted on paper, mounted on cloth. There were masonic devices, emblematic monsters, wonderfully shaped spangles, roses, wreaths, and other caprices of the imagination of the Scarsdale artists. The result was one of barbaric splendour of colour and tinsel. This marvellous pomp was heralded by a deafening clamour of the band, which did its worst against rival sounds, even almost drowning the frantic shouts with which the phenomenon of the banner was greeted. Seth Diggle had been promoted to the post of honour on the top of the cart, where he held a banner on which the Scarsdale arms were emblazoned on the Union Jack. Before the cart was started for Rochdale, however, a country-dance was formed on each side of the road, it being the privilege of the young men yoked in the cart to choose their partners from the prettiest country girls—nothing loth for such a distinction. The band struck up loudly, the banners stood grandly at one end of the two sets of thirty couples, and at the other the cart, with Seth in the bower at its crown. Half-an-hour was devoted to this dance, when the bugle again sounded, the dance at once ceased, the young men kissed their partners and took their places, and, amidst the shouts of the crowd, and the wildest efforts of the band, the Scarsdale rush-cart started for Rochdale. About the same time a similar fête was in progress at Hurstwood, at Martinmere, at Eastleton, at Milnrow, at Smallbridge, at Whitworth, at Spotland, and other villages, for it was the glory of Rochdale to assemble at its rush-bearing, forty years ago, at least eight, and sometimes a dozen, rush-carts from the neighbouring villages. Meanwhile the gala of the rush-bearing was in the delirium of its frenzy, the rush carts having assembled in the street opposite the Butts, each with its band in front, the order of procession extending over the bridge across the Roche, and a considerable distance up Yorkshire Street. Every band played with stentorian energy, 'Rule Britannia;' the young men drawing every cart vied with each other in the vigour and picturesque character of their dances, the flags in every bower on the top of the rush-carts were waved triumphantly, the spangled and decorated banners carried before each band glittered in the bright noon, from every window hung flags or coloured draperies, handkerchiefs were waved, and loud huzzas broke to swell the exulting torrent of acclamation. The main thoroughfares were crowded by a multitude of folk in their gayest dresses. In side-streets were stalls with Eccles cakes, Everton toffy, and Ormskirk gingerbread, and booths with shows of every kind frequenting a country fair. Conjurers stood on their stages, watching for the passage of the procession, to attract a crowd of gazers by their wonderful tricks. Mountebanks and clowns were ready to perform when the streets were clear from the grand pageant of the day. There was a bear on the Butts, growling defiance at the dogs by which it was to be baited, and climbing at intervals to the top of the high stake to which he was chained. Then a pilot balloon of gay colours floated gracefully from a garden of the 'Orchard,' near the river, and the roar of guns boomed on the ear at short intervals as the pretty phantom rose in the still air to a great height and then floated away in the tide of an upper current. When the twenty-first gun had been fired, the procession commenced its progress through the town."

It is pleasing to turn from the noisy account just given to the quaint little scene on the following page, which illustrates some remarks on the custom by the author of the "Pictorial History of Lancashire":[*]

"Almost every village or hamlet within six miles of Bury has its rush-bearing. The custom is easily accounted for; the churches formerly having neither boards nor flags, and the floor being composed of clay, well trodden down, rushes were therefore strewed on

[*] 1844, pp. 249-250.

the aisles to prevent them being too cold, hence the taking away the
old rushes and bringing in fresh ones grew at last quite into a
periodical festival. A well-built rush-cart is very difficult to accom-
plish, and the whole pageant itself is a very picturesque sight. First
come the band of musicians, all gaily dressed, and a smart new
banner with some quaint device upon it; then the fool or half-wit of
the village, dressed in the most absurd manner possible, generally a
cocked hat, scarlet hunting-coat and boots, sword in hand, and
mounted on a donkey; then the cart with the rushes built in a
peculiar fashion like the roof of a house, the gable being to the front,
and sloping down over the wheels, beautifully cut, the edges being
closely shaved, and the triangular space in front adorned with rosettes
of ribbon, and streamers, tinsel ornaments, and even *watches*. The
top is surmounted with a small flag or banner, and astride of all,

A BURY RUSH-CART.

holding the said banner, a little boy or a young man, sometimes both.
The cart is drawn by thirty or forty young men, two and two, holding
high above their heads poles, which are fastened by ropes on each
side to the cart, there being to each pole about half-a-dozen bells.
The young men, and in fact all the persons forming the procession,
are most gaily dressed, the favourite style being straw hats with light
blue ribbons, white shirt sleeves tied with many-coloured ribbons, the
brightest handkerchiefs possible for sashes, * and ribbons again below
the knee. The cart and its drawers are flanked by ten or twelve
similarly dressed countrymen, each with a huge new cart whip, which

* The brilliantly-striped silk scarves known as "Mogadors" were in great
demand for this purpose.

they ply lustily about, and crack loudly in time to the merry tune of the musicians.

"There are but slight differences in the detail of the rush-bearings in other villages. At Rochdale, the neighbourhood being very populous, there are sometimes eight or nine rush-carts, each having its band, etc., and they not infrequently meet in one of the narrow streets, when generally a pretty stout battle takes place for precedence, as it is well-known that those who arrive the first at the church always receive a donation of five shillings. It must not be supposed that these processions *occur* on the Sabbath day, the rushes are procured *for* the Sunday, but the procession usually takes place a few days before, the dates of each rush-bearing being calculated by the Sunday previous. Instead of men, horses now frequently draw the cart, and in most places the rushes are sold after the festivity, which, from having no small portion of a religious character, has degenerated into a mere holiday-making.

"Connected with rush-bearings, there is what is called the Skedlock-Cart,* used by children in a small cart, wagon, or wheel-barrow, made of the yellow flowers of the large weed, charlock, kedlack, or cadlock, in imitation of the rush-cart."

These "skedlock-carts" used to be common enough about Gorton twenty-five years ago. They were generally made by children, in a small box set on wheels. This was filled up with rushes, grass, or docks, but always covered at the top with rushes, laid lengthways, the ends being to the front and back. These were tied on with string, and in the top thus made were stuck any kind of wild flowers that could be got, charlock, buttercups, daisies, meadow-sweet, etc. The children's hats were dressed with flowers, rush-whips, and small thorn twigs, on the thorns of which flowers were stuck, were carried in the hand, a larger branch being sometimes stuck in the centre of the cart. On one occasion I saw one of these carts on which sat astride a small child, just able to walk, its hat covered with flowers, a bunch of buttercups in one hand, and a stick of "swaggering dick" (with which its face was smeared) in the other. The girls drawing

* Skedlock, Kedlock, Keddledock, and Kettledock, is a name given in Lancashire to the common ragwort (*Senecio jacobea*), and also to charlock (*sinapis arvensis*).

the cart had adorned their hats with flowers, whilst the boys improvised music out of tin whistles and old cans. These carts were not made at the rush-bearing only, but at any time during the summer when flowers could be got.

In August, 1874, some children at Levenshulme had a small rush-cart, and its train of morris-dancers.

Skedlock-carts are yet to be met with in the hill districts of South-East Lancashire, the children going round with an imitation rush-cart in a small box or wheelbarrow, and collecting money to spend at the wakes. They were to be seen at Saddleworth this year (1890). The accompanying plate shows a skedlock-cart made entirely by boys at Uppermill in 1879. It was very neatly built of rushes in a hand-cart, had the "bolts" adorned with flowers, and the sheet in front covered with tinsel and artificial flowers. The larger boys upheld the shafts, whilst a long rope enabled the smaller ones to assist in drawing. There were the green boughs at the top, on which a boy rode astride, a fifer and a drummer, a boy with a whip, and the inevitable collecting-boxes. The whole formed a complete rush-bearing in miniature.

At Didsbury, the rush-cart, followed by the morris-dancers, went round the hamlets of Burnage and Heaton Norris at the beginning of August. The custom was continued until the Rev. W. Kidd came to Didsbury as incumbent, when it was discontinued on account of the objections urged by that and other gentlemen in the parish.

The four townships of Newton Heath, Moston, Failsworth, and Droylsden, near Manchester, having only one church among them (that at Newton Heath), formerly joined in a rush-cart, which went round each township once in four years. The rush-bearing was held from time immemorial on the Friday before the Sunday following the 18th of

August. Droylsden has since ceased to have any connection with the other three (which still have their wakes at the same time), and no longer keeps its wakes on the day held by the others. As Moston, Failsworth, and Newton Heath each have now a church of their own, great irregularity has prevailed for some years in the rush-bearings, as there being no rush-cart one year, and two or three the next. Failsworth took the lead in this festivity, and their rush-cart, always the largest, best dressed, and bearing the most valuable plate, used frequently to extend their peregrinations to Manchester. One such promenaded the streets on Tuesday evening, 25th August, 1874. Heading the procession was a drum and fife band, followed by a troop of about twenty morris-dancers attired in fantastic costumes, and wearing hats covered with flowers. After these came the rush-cart, drawn by nine gaily-trapped horses. The rush-stack was an exceedingly large one, weighing about three tons. At the top were seated two men, who were surrounded by green boughs and Union Jacks, whilst in front was a fine display of silver cups, plates, etc. Behind the cart were several men with boxes for contributions from the spectators. At times the streets were completely blocked by the crowd of sightseers.

Droylsden's rush-cart was always fabricated at Greenside, and in 1793, John Wood, of Clayton Hall Farm, provided rushes, waggon, and eight stump-tailed horses to draw it from that hamlet to Newton. Few complete brass bands were then in existence, but, by gleaning in Gorton, Manchester, and other places, an extemporised company of instrumentalists was formed. Owing to dissensions in 1817, a rush-cart was made at the "White Hart," in opposition to the orthodox pageant at Greenside. The rush-cart manufactured in Droylsden in 1855, perambulated the village, and patronised Manchester, but did not visit

Newton at all. In a waggon or cart was constructed a coned and symmetrical pyramid, faced with bolts of green rushes, and filled up with dried ones, and was decorated with ribbons, flowers, and a glittering display of silver plate. The procession was headed by the chapel garland.*

From the MS., published and unpublished, of the late John Higson, we are enabled to gather many particulars of the rush-bearing at Gorton, a village near Manchester, long celebrated for its breed of bulldogs, its sturdy men, and its wakes. In 1775, the Openshaw rush-bearing to Gorton Chapel was discontinued. About 1780, the rush-cart went out on the Friday before the first Sunday in September, perambulating the village, visiting Mr. Grimshaw's, High Bank, and also the locality of Gorton Brook. On that night, or Saturday morning, the rushes were "teemed" down near the chapel gates. The old ones of last year having been cleared out of the chapel, the new ones were carried in, and carefully strewn in the bottom of the pews, aisles, etc. On this day, also, the band, accompanied by the "pikemen" carrying staves surmounted with brass eagles, perambulated the village, stopping nowhere, neither soliciting nor receiving any contributions. The garlands which had adorned the rush-bearing were placed in the chapel, they were suspended on staves, which were fastened to the pillars in front of the lofts [galleries], where they remained till the next anniversary, when they were removed to make room for their successors, and although they somewhat intercepted the view of a portion of those who sat in the galleries, yet no complaints were ever made. On the Sunday the morris-dancers, and other officials connected with the rush-bearing, all attended the chapel, when an appropriate sermon was preached.

* Higson's "History of Droylsden," 1859, pp. 65-66.

This day finished the wake, labour being everywhere resumed on the Monday.

1800. The wake was held, and the rush-cart made alternately at Edward Stannings, the "Horse and Farrier," Bottom o' th' Brow, and William Shawcross, the "George and Dragon" (now Chapel House).

1804. At this time much attention was devoted to the annual rush-bearing. Early on this auspicious morning, James Hibbert, of Fox Fold, and his assistants, might be observed preparing the rushes, and whilst they were erecting the pyramid, and decking it out with silver plate, garlands, etc., the morris-dancers were as eagerly decking themselves in their holiday attire, and neatly covering their clean white shirts and light "senglits" with various-hued ribbons, neckbeads, and other trinkets. Choice horses were selected to convey the rush-cart, the Gorton Band accompanied the procession, and the dancers, in couples, tripped it on the "light fantastic toe" to the tune of the "Morris-dance," etc. It was customary for the cart to perambulate the heart of the village; it afterwards proceeded to the out-skirts, and on the Saturday was dismantled. There was generally a bear-bait under Fox Fold, commencing at six A.M., and renewed at intervals of three or four hours until nightfall. Bear and badger-baits were held on the vacant land opposite the "Black Horse," Bottom o' th' Brow, and bull-baits at the "George and Dragon."

1805. Joseph Bradshaw, of Whiteley Cottages, Gorton, the rush-cart maker, died, aged sixty-two, and was succeeded by James Hibbert, of Fox Fold.

1829. At the wake this year there were five bull-baits in or near the village, viz., at the "Plough Inn," "Chapel House," "Lamb Tavern," Marchington's "Abbey Hey," and the "Bull's Head," Aspinall Smithy; and a bear-bait at the "Black Horse." The rush-cart, as usual, after perambulating the village, proceeded to

Manchester. Ultimately, when the band and morris-dancers were half-seas over, they entered Newton Lane (the Irish pale). The former commenced the tune of "Croppy lie down," instantly the war-whoop was sounded, and hundreds of the "boys" immediately commenced an unequal war on the rash and unfortunate offenders. The assailants were armed with brooms, pokers, tongs, knobsticks, etc.; the musicians turned their instruments into implements of war and defence, music for once having failed to charm the savage breast. The dancers tript their light fantastic toes, *Lancashire fashion*, upon the posteriors of their opponents. The rush-cart was mounted by two Irishmen; the drivers, alarmed for the safety of the plate which adorned it, lashed their horses; one scalader contrived to escape, but the other was detained, and driven to Gorton in gallant style, and upon him the Gortonians wreaked their fury. The old fool wisely enough turned his regalia, an old broom, into a weapon of offence and defence. Many of the dancers, being nimble of foot, commenced a speedy retreat, recollecting that

"He who fights and runs away
Will live to fight another day."

At intervals throughout the day, "odd dancers" might be seen stealthily approaching the village, covered with wounds and glory, their dresses, plumes, and ribbons woefully dishevelled and torn. Since this period the rush-bearing at Gorton has gradually declined.

1832. "Paid 3s. for posting up bills as a caution for and against the wakes."

1839. A rush-cart, made at Mr. Chadwick's, under the auspices of Mr. Bennett, of Gorton Hall. It was richly adorned with festoons of flowers, garlands, and silver plate, and accompanied by the Gorton Band. After visiting the hall, etc., they proceeded to Man-

SADDLEWORTH RUSHBEARING.

chester, Mr. Bennett paying the toll over Blackfriar's Bridge.

1841. A rush-cart was made at the "Waggon and Horses," under the superintendence of Mr. Bennett. One of the metallic ornaments consisted of a handsome gold cup, won by one of Mr. Bennett's greyhounds in a coursing match. The rush-cart visited the hall, and paraded the village, and then went to Manchester, where the dancers were liberally treated.

1842. Mr. James Stopford purchased, at Mrs. Taylor's sale, Reddish, the bells formerly worn by the horses drawing Gorton rush-cart.

1851. A small rush-cart made at the "Chapel House." It was drawn by three horses, decorated with bells. The pyramid of rushes, however, was destitute of ornament, either of flowers or silver plate. It was surmounted by two men amongst oak branches. The procession was headed by a banner, the fool, men cracking long whips, etc. The band were dressed in uniform, and were accompanied by about ten couples of morris-dancers. Amongst the procession were several with alms boxes, the funds collected being spent in drink.

After this time, the rush-cart was only made at intervals, although the wakes was held as usual, now and again bursting out into something like its old splendour. On the 9th September, 1874, a rush-cart was made in the old style. The morris-dancers (or "molly-dancers," as they are now often called by the ignorant), were led by the fool, who bore the title of "King Coffee" inscribed on his hat. "The dancers made a very pleasing march, wheeling round with a sort of salute, and falling into two lines facing each other. Their dress was remarkably gay, and in good taste. It was almost a copy of the dress of Spanish dancers or bull-fighters. Red or blue 'shorts,' or knee-breeches, long stockings, gaily coloured sashes over their full shirts, with plenty of brooches and other ornaments about chest and neck, straw hats piled high with flowers, and curious long knotted skeins of cotton hanging from their wrists, which the dancers used somewhat in the way of castanets. The dance was gone through with remarkable precision, and even gracefulness. The procession was aided by two men carrying long carter's whips, and followed by the famous old rush-cart."*

About a week before the wakes a number of boys in the neighbourhood go about collecting money. Four of them, two at each end, carry a pole, astride of which sits a boy with his face blacked, his coat turned inside out, or else wearing an old one torn to ribbons, and altogether dressed as outrageously as possible. They form a procession, headed by other boys with tin whistles and cans, and on arriving at a house sing the old rush-cart song.

"In the course of the year," says Edwin Waugh, † "there are two very ancient festivals which are kept up, each with its own quaint peculiarities, by the Heywood people, and commemorated by them with general rejoicing and cessation from labour. One of these is the 'Rush-bearing,' held in the month of August, an old feast which seems to have died out almost everywhere else in England, except in Lancashire. Here, in Heywood, however, as in many other towns of the county, this ancient ceremony is still observed, with two or three days' holiday, hilarity, and feasting, in the hay season."

In a letter to Browne Willis, 22nd November, 1726, from the Hon. H. Egerton, of Heaton, near Prestwich, ‡ the latter says: "I am making what enquiry I can as to Dedication of Churches, but there being few such festivals as Wakes observed in this Neighbourhood,

---

* "Manchester Guardian."—Notes and Queries, No. 456.
† "Sketches of Lancashire Life and Localities," 1857, p. 168.
‡ Willis MSS., vol. xxxv., f. 359, Bodleian Library.

we shall be, I doubt, defective. As to ours of Prestwich, we have nothing but a Custom of bringing Rushes to Church in a cart, with great Ceremony, Dancing before it, and Cart and horses adorned with Plate, Ribbons, and Garlands. The time anciently and usually observed is about St. Bartholomew's Day [25th August], whenever 'tis supposed its dedication is to ye Saint. They have Wakes at Eccles and Ratclyffe, but at the last of no long-standing, unless formerly lay'd aside and lately revived."

Manchester had no rush-cart of its own, but every year a number of carts visited the town from the outtownships, some coming as far as from Oldham and Rochdale. They were always looked forward to, and liberally treated, and the inhabitants had thus the opportunity of inspecting the rival carts, and criticising the proficiency or otherwise of the morris-dancers who accompanied them. The accompanying view of such a scene is taken from a fine picture, painted by Alexander Wilson, in 1821 (formerly in the possession of Mr. Roger Wilson, of Woodford, Cheshire), representing a rush-cart in Long Millgate, Manchester.[*] The canvas is studded with characteristic figures, inclusive of the artist himself (his bandaged foot requiring temporary crutches), the Rev. Joshua Brookes, and Gentleman Cooper, the tall, enthusiastic pedestrian who walked to Doncaster and home again, during forty successive years, for the pleasure of witnessing the exciting race for the St. Leger stakes. In addition to these, there is Mr. John Ogden, the grocer, vignetted through his shop window, and a full-length portly boniface in the centre, Mr. Henry Slater, of the "Bay Horse Tavern." In the heart of the crowd a sweep, astride on a pig, upsets a man engaged in carrying beer who in turn capsizes an optician bearing a weather-

[*] Reproduced also in Procter's "Memorials of Manchester Streets," 1874, pp. 36-37.

glass marked "much rain." Taking advantage of the uproar, a thief is abstracting from the pocket of a dandy a packet of *billet doux*. Some of the curious devices borne at the rush-bearing are depicted, and it is noticeable that the morris-dancers are represented in trousers instead of knee-breeches, and wearing the curious helmet-shaped hats occasionally worn by morris-dancers, instead of straw hats. Wilson's picture perpetuates a scene that was of very frequent occurrence in Manchester during a long series of years. But the Irish, taking offence at some orange-coloured lilies adorning a rush-cart, fell upon the dancers and dispersed them, a proceeding which occurred on several subsequent occasions, and led to a discontinuance of the visits of the rush-carts.

On the 31st August, 1882, a rush-cart from Oldham came to Manchester, and paraded the principal streets about five o'clock in the afternoon. It was made in an ordinary two-wheeled cart. The angles were feathered, and formed of rods about an inch thick, the tops projecting about a foot, and painted blue. On the top of the cart, almost hidden by a great bough of oak, was a little man with a very dirty face, and wearing a red jacket. The sides of the cart were plain, on the back, "V.R.," formed of yellow flowers stuck in the rushes. The front was covered with a clean white cloth, on which were fastened several watches, a tea-urn, and three large silver salvers, besides several silver cups, cream jugs, a teapot, and spoons. The cart was drawn by a grey horse in the shafts, decorated with flowers and ribbands. From the ends of the shafts were two long ropes, kept apart by seven "swingle-trees," or "stretchers" (wooden poles which keep the chains asunder behind a chain-horse), to each of which were three young men, dressed in their every-day clothes. These assisted the horse in drawing. There was a band of music, a banner, and then five boys dressed

THE RUSH-CART.

up, two with straw hats trimmed with flowers, the other three with large caps resembling helmets (as shown below), formed of laths, and covered with ribbons and rosettes. They had knotted handkerchiefs tied to their wrists, and danced the morris to the two usual rush-cart tunes. There were, also, a boy with a wooden box to receive money, and a great carter, armed with an immense whip, who preceded the procession and produced a series of loud cracks with his whip. There was no fool.

MORRIS-DANCER'S HAT.

Rochdale, being an ancient market town, and the centre of a number of populous villages, probably saw more rush-carts in its streets at one time than any other place in England, eight or nine being a not infrequent number at wakes time, and, as the streets were narrow, collisions between rival rush-carts were frequent. Local jealousies, party-strife, and often an inclination to have a fight for supremacy led to much disorder, and more than once downright bloodshed. The ill-feeling

between the Whigs and Jacobites at the time of the
Scotch rebellion, in 1745, lasted for some years, and
often broke out into riot. On the 20th August, 1748,
Adam Robinson brought an action at the Lancaster
Assizes, in the Court of King's Bench, against James
Ramsbottom and Abraham Lowton, for trespass, which
affords a glimpse at the manners of the time. Robinson complained that in 1747, at Rochdale, Ramsbottom
and Lowton, with sticks, stones, and staves, and force
of arms, attacked his dwelling-house, called the "Union
Flagg Inn," in Rochdale, broke 100 panes of glass,
and other wrong did to the damage of £10.

"It is usual at Rochdale to have a sort of Feast
every year in August, called the Rush-bearing, when
the Fools and Populace of one Township in the Parish
vie with another in the strength of their Mob or Party,
the shew of their Garlands, and such nonsense, and
since the Rebellion they've Distinguished themselves,
by the Aid and Genius of a certain Justice of the Peace
in the Neighbourhood, into two Parties, called *Blacks*
and *Jacks*, i.e., *Whigs* and *Tories*. On the 10th
August, 1747, the Blacks, not content with making
their show in the streets only, attacked Mr. Robinson's
house, pretending some of the Jacks were drinking
there, and about eleven o'clock at night several scores
of 'em, assisted by some recruiting soldiers, broke
open the house, and cast many stones out of the street
in at the windows, and wounded several people of the
house within, and, after insulting and threatening the
plaintiff and his family, ransacked and plundered the
house, and committed great enormities. The aid of
the civil power was called in, and the mob dispersed.

"A witness deposed that he saw a *Plaid* handkerchief hung out of the window. Garlands dressed up
with orange-coloured ribbons not liked, and 'down
with the Rump' was the word, when the garlands were

A LANCASHIRE RUSH-CART.

demolished. A song was sung in praise of the Duke of Cumberland, when stones and piss-pots were thrown from the Union balcony. A man almost killed, Union house disaffected and abusive, mob loyal," etc. *

In Jesse Lee's copy of Baines's "History of Lancashire," now in the Public Reference Library, Manchester,† is the following draft of a letter to Hone's "Year Book,"‡ dated 4th May, 1825. It differs somewhat from that given by Hone, and the latter's woodcut, represented on page 67, bears little resemblance to the sketches sent, which we reproduce on pages 69, 70, and 72. He writes :

"As the celebration of the Wakes are now approaching, I beg leave to send you a brief account of them, or, as they are called in this part of Lancashire, Rush-bearings, the origin of which I had explained to me by a very old person who died several years ago, who stated that in his remembrance (before Parish Churches were paved, or rendered more comfortable by the use of stoves and the present method of heating and ventilating), rushes were brought by persons out of the country in bundles, adorned with flowers, ribbons, etc., some very plain and others tastefully decorated with garlands, for which the parties received a small acknowledgment from the churchwardens. These rushes were put into the churchyard, spread, and regularly turned until sufficiently dry to be taken into the church, the bottom of which was strewed, and which served to keep the feet of the congregation from being chilled by the pavement, and, in some instances, by a clay floor. The improvements in Manufacture and Commerce since then having rendered the working-class more refined and luxurious, hath almost done away with the old method of rush-bearing, and the present system of building not requiring the aid of rushes, the Feasts are celebrated by the display of rushes in carts, most tastefully formed, of which the sketch I send may convey a better idea than a long description. Some are drawn by horses, gaily dressed, but they are more general[ly] drawn by the young men, § preceded by music and a banner, some of which I have seen four or five yards broad by six or eight long, ‖ composed of silk of various

---

* Raines MSS., vol. xiv., pp. 438-441, Chetham Library.
† Vol. ii., pt. 3, p. 635.
‡ See the "Year Book," 1832, pp. 552-556.
§ "To the number of twenty or thirty couple, profusely adorned with ribands, tinsel, etc."—"Year Book."
‖ "Having on either side, in the centre, a painting of Britannia, the king's arms, or some other device."—"Year Book."

colours, joined together by fretwork of narrow ribbon, and profusely covered with roses, stars, and fringes of tinsel,* which, when viewed, dazzles the eye of the beholder if the sun shines upon it. The procession is preceded and flanked by a number of men with long cart whips, which are in continual action of cracking, and causes a clear path, † after which, a number of men with horse-bells about them, jumping grotesquely and jingling the bells, after them, the band, and sometimes a number of young men as Morris-dancers, ‡ followed by young women bearing garlands, and, lastly, the cart ; upon the front of the same is a white cloth, covered entirely with plate, such as cups, tankards, spoons, and watches. § Great rivalry exists between the young men of the neighbouring villages which shall produce the best-formed cart and banner, and it not infrequently happens that when

A. *Staves attached to the ropes for the men to draw by, generally two abreast, sometimes as many as from 20 to 30 couples*

two of the processions meet in the street a conflict takes place, and many bloody noses made. A contribution from the different in

---

* "Which in this part is called 'horse gold.'"—"Ibid." A name by which it is yet (1890) known in Saddleworth.

† "Some thirty years ago, the advent of Rush-bearing was marked by the cracking of whips. These whips were made of rope and string, the lash being five feet long, and the handle about eighteen inches, and, when skilfully used, the result was a crack as loud as a pistol shot."—Fishwick's "History of Rochdale," 1889, p. 533. There was also another kind often used, having long heavy handles and lashes, requiring the use of both hands, and more difficult to use than the first-named.

‡ "But without the ancient appendage of bells."—"Year Book."

§ "Rushes are laid transversely on the rush-cart, and are cut by sharp knives to the form desired, in which no little art is required. The bolts, as they are termed, are formed of the largest rushes, tied up in bundles of about two inches in diameter. These bolts are, as the work of making proceeds, affixed to rods fixed in the four corners of the cart, and carved to the form required. When the cart is finished, the load of rushes is decorated with carnations and other flowers, in different devices, and surmounted by branches of oak, and a person rides on the top."—"Year Book."

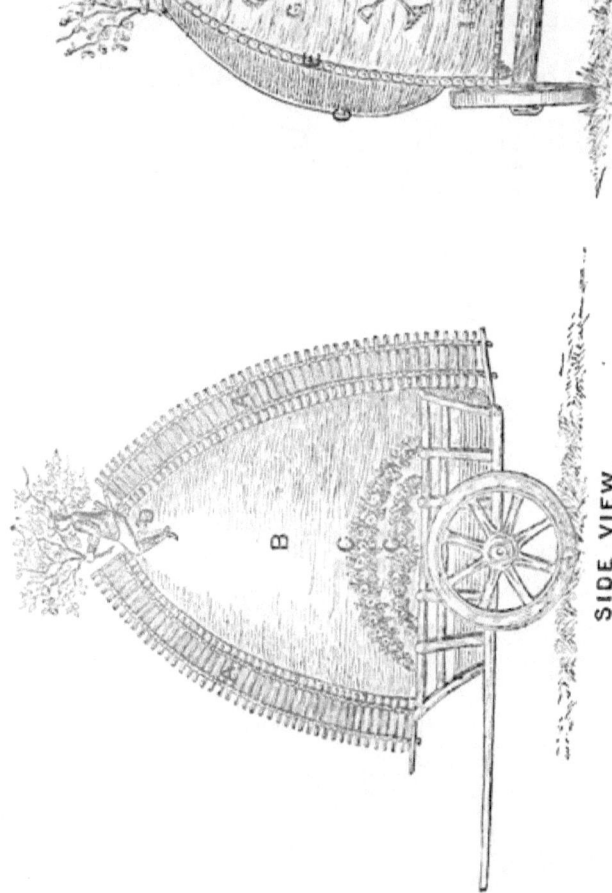

habitants enables the parties to sacrifice at the shrine of Sir John Barleycorn, which is continued for several days. These Rush-bearings . . . are generally held in the months of July, August, and September. . . . Rochdale Rush-bearing commences on the 3d Sunday in August. I have seen six or seven carts on one day, viz., on the Monday from Newbold, Lowerplace, Bagslate, Marland, Milkstone, Broad Lane, Spotland, Smallbridge, etc. The Rush-bearings round this part are Ripponden, Ashworth, Littleboro, Milnrow, Rochdale, Heywood, Oldham, Royton, Shaw Chapel, Whitworth, and Middleton, at which places the customs are much alike.

"The person who forms and cuts the rushes is called the 'featherer.' It was a featherer who was one of the persons unfortunately shot at the riot in this town (April, 1796, I believe),* in memory of which the men who drew the Marland cart, for a number of years after, each wore a black scarf; but it is now discontinued. There is a remarkable anecdote in the 'Imperial Magazine,' 1822, vol. iv., col. 1203, respecting the fate of the above two men."

"The rush-bearing is now (1820)," writes Canon Raines,† "on the Monday after the third Sunday in August. Formerly, it began on the Saturday immediately preceding the third Sunday, but, owing to the dissipated scenes which were witnessed on the Sunday, Dr. Hind, about 1780, forbad the rushes to be brought to the church on the Saturday,‡ and also forbad the usual notice to be given to the parishioners to bring

---

* In Sir Samuel Rush-Meyrick's letter to Mr. George Shaw, already quoted, he speaks of this occurrence as "an accident at Rochdale, on Easter Monday, in 1794 or 5 (but qy. 1793)." The riot, however, which took place through a scarcity of bread, occurred on the 5th August, 1795, and the circumstances were as follows: A practice formerly prevailed at Rochdale for the men of the town to play football with the men of the neighbouring country places, which seldom ended without a quarrel. In one of these disputes, about the year 1745, a man named C——, from Marland, four miles from Rochdale, killed a man belonging to the latter place; but, as no proper evidence could be obtained of the fact, he escaped without prosecution. Some time after, he left Rochdale, and went to reside at Congleton, in Cheshire. There he heard the Gospel, and became converted. After a lapse of fifty years, he went on a visit to Rochdale to see a relation. On the Monday after his arrival he walked down to the bridge. Some disturbance happening that morning, the volunteers were ordered out, and were drawn up on the bridge, and as C—— was shaking hands with an old acquaintance, who had been present in the former fray when the man was killed, they received orders to fire. C—— and his old acquaintance both fell, the former dead, the latter surviving a short time. These were the only men who lost their lives, and, as near as possible, where the man fell whom C—— killed.

† Raines MSS., vol. xiv., p. 438, Chetham Library.

‡ He also prohibited the carts being introduced into the churchyard, to the great displeasure of sundry important personages.

SKETCH OF THE GENERAL APPEARANCE OF A BANNER WHICH IS CARRIED BY MEN UPON A NUMBER OF REEDS TIED TOGETHER.

the rushes, which, from an early period, had been proclaimed by the sexton, standing on a tombstone, immediately after evening service, the Sunday preceding the Rush-bearing."

About the year 1868, the late James Dearden, Esq., of Rochdale, finding that no rush-carts then came to Rochdale, offered a prize of ten guineas for the most handsome that came, five guineas for the next best, and one guinea for each that came. About twenty appeared, and a number also turned up the following year.

Bishop Gastrel,* in 1717, alludes to "the disorderly custom called Rush-bearing (at Milnrow) on Saturday next before St. James's Day." The church is dedicated to St. James. At Milnrow, the feast is sufficiently near St. Bartholomew's Day to point out its origin.

"1617, July 25th, St. James Day.—At Whalley, ther a rush-bearing, but much less solemnitie than formerly."—Journal of Nicholas Assheton.† The Rev. Canon Raines adds :

"Prior to 1636 there are now no accounts at Whalley, and no reference to the custom is made till 1700, after which time there are regular entries every year for cleansing the church. 'St. pd. for Dressing ye Church against St. James' Day, 05s. 00d.' The rushes were brought on the rush cart, by the north gate, into the church, free of expense. Garlands were suspended in the church, and on the top of the steeple. It is about seventy years since the floor of Whalley Church was strewed with rushes ; and after the occasion for its use ceased, the rush-cart soon disappeared, though the festival itself was kept up, and the morris-dancers played their part in it, for more than twenty years afterwards. Not fifty years since, on the 5th of August, the village was crowded like a fair ; booths were erected, and horse races, and other rustic sports, attracted numbers of people from the surrounding country. The late R. Grimshaw Lomax, Esq., was in the habit of staying at Whalley, on the 5th August, on his annual return from Stonyhurst 'Academy Day,' and, along with Mr. Adam Cottam, endeavoured to keep alive the taste for old English

* "Notitia Cestriensis," vol. i., p. 216.
† Chetham Society, 1848, pp. 29-30.

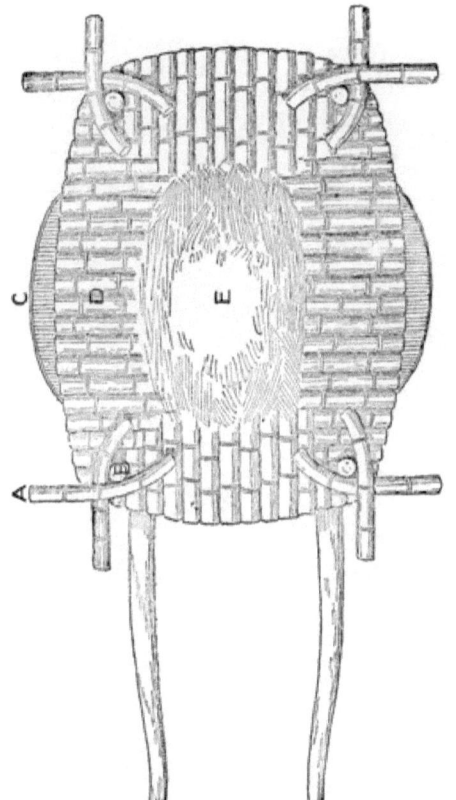

PLAN of RUSHCART.

A. The edges of "featherings" formed of small bundles of rushes about 2 inches thick.
B. Rods set up in the angles to give shape and strength.
C. Iron of featherings over the wheel.
D. Long handles of rushes, the ties bearing smoothly cut.
E. Loose rushes to fill up the cart, well trodden down.

GREENFIELD RUSHCART.

sport; but the festival gradually declined, and within the last two years St. James' Day, the rush-cart, and the festival, have altogether ceased in Whalley. It may be observed that St. James' Day, old style, would be on the 6th August, and the rush-bearing, the 5th of August, would therefore be the Eve of St. James."

The custom of rush-bearing was not so elaborately nor so enthusiastically observed in Cheshire as in Lancashire, though in its main features the same, and is now almost obsolete. Ormerod * describes :

"The great and peculiar feature of the festival [the wakes] as the rush-bearing, which is still in use in many parts of the county. This ceremony [as in use at Lymm, in 1817] consists of carrying to church the rushes intended to be strewed on the clay floor under the benches, which are piled neatly up in a cart, and a person constantly attends to pare the edges with a hay knife, if disordered in progress. The cart and the horses are carefully selected from the various village teams, and decorated with flowers and ribbands, and on the rushes sit persons holding garlands, intended to ornament the church for the year ensuing. These are composed of hoops slung round a pole, connected by cross strings, which are concealed by artificial flowers, cut paper, and tinsel. One is placed in the rector's, or principal, chancel, and the others in the subordinate ones belonging to the several manor-houses of the parish, and they are frequently ornamented by the young ladies of the respective mansions. The cart, thus loaded, goes round to the neighbouring seats, preceded by male and female Morris-Dancers, who perform a peculiar dance at each house, and are attended by a man in female attire (something between the fool and the Maid Maryan), who jingles a bell to the tune, and holds a large wooden ladle for money. As night approaches, the cart, with its attendants, returns to the town where the church is situated, and there the garlands are fixed, whilst a peal is rung on the bells, and the concourse of village revellers is attracted to view the spectacle."

In Coles MSS., preserved in the Harleian Collection, British Museum, there is an account of a rush-bearing at Bunbury, dated 30th July, 1755 :

"Being at my worthy Friend, the Rev. Mr. Allen's, house, at Tarporley, and hearing that there was a famous Rush-bearing, as the Cheshire people call it [to be held at Bunbury], on account of the hanging up of a new Chandelier of Brass in the Church, which cost

* "History of Cheshire," 2nd edition, 1882, vol. i., pp. 81-2.

the Parish about Thirty-Pounds, we took a ride there in the evening to see the ceremony.

"This parish is a very large one, and has about a dozen Townships depending on it, which all send, at different times, Garlands and large kind of Fans, adorned with gilt paper cut into various figures, and mixed with Flowers. These were borne by separate persons, each having one in his hand, and coming in procession from their different Townships, at intervals; and many of the neighbouring villages, also, sending them Garlands, all which were set up in different parts of the Church, made it look very ornamental, and gave the whole village an air of gaiety and cheerfulness not usual in the more Southerly parts of the Kingdom.

"On the Dedication Day of their Churches in the North, it is usual to strew them with rushes, and otherwise adorn them; but it had not being practiced at Bunbury within the memory of man. But, having new-roofed their Church about two years before, and very handsomely cieled it, and buying the aforesaid brass Branch, they were desirous of solemnising the memory of it, and the day following was to be ushered in with Ringing of Bells, and two Sermons, and great Psalm-singing, and other Festivities. St. Boniface is the Patron Saint of the Church, on which day their Wake is held."

At Christleton Rush-bearing in July, 1810, one of the principal attractions was a bull-bait.

Holt, on the Dee, formerly had the floor of its church strewn with rushes; and Wrexham was celebrated for its rush-bearing, in which its celebrated ale bore no inconsiderable part.

In the parishes of Farndon, Holt, Aldford, Coddington, Tilstone, Isacoed, Gresford, and Harthill, they have a custom which has not, I believe, been noticed elsewhere, that of "hilling" or decorating the graves and tombstones with rushes and flowers, in addition to dressing the church. The day observed is the 16th July, or the first Sunday after, formerly the first Sunday after Midsummer Day (old style).

In Chambers's "Book of Days," * it is stated that "in Cheshire, at Runcorn and Warburton, the annual rush-bearing wake is carried out in grand style. A large quantity of rushes, sometimes a cart-load, is

---

* 1863, vol. i., p. 506.

UPPERMILL RUSHCART. 1889.

collected, and, being bound on the cart, are cut evenly at each end, and on Saturday evening a number of men sit on the top of the rushes, holding garlands of artificial flowers, tinsel, etc. The cart is drawn round the parish by three or four spirited horses, decked with ribbons, the collars being surrounded with small bells. It is attended by morris-dancers, fantastically dressed. There are men dressed in women's clothes, one of whom, with his face blackened, has a belt, with a large bell attached, round his waist, and carries a ladle to collect money from the spectators. The party stop and dance at the public-houses in their way to the parish church, where the rushes are deposited, and the garlands are hung up, to remain till the next year." The custom is now discontinued.

At Forest Chapel, near Macclesfield, the little church is usually crowded on the rush-bearing Sunday. Until a comparatively recent period the floor of Wincle Church was neither paved nor flagged, but spread with rushes. These were renewed annually, on a certain Sunday in July, when it was customary to decorate a cart with flowers, and bear them to church. This was celebrated with great rejoicing, and was termed the "rush-bearing;" and in after years, when rushes were no longer used, the drinking and name were still kept up, but they are now wisely discontinued. The "wake," entirely distinct from the rush-bearing, still recurs annually, though somewhat on the decline.*

Finney, in his MS. "History of the Parish of Wilmslow," written c. 1780, thus alludes to the custom in that village:

"In order to ornament the church for this festival (that of the wakes or dedication), there is a custom called a Rush-bearing, for two townships, in their turns, to bring in a cart-load of Rushes, nicely dressed and ornamented with flowers, on the Saturday but one preceding the festival. They often vie with each other in finery, in morrice-dancing,

---

* "The Reliquary," vol. v., p. 3.

and in tinsel, painted paper, and flower garlands. The Rushes are spread upon the floors in the farmers' pews and between the benches, and serve to keep their feet warm in winter, and to kneel upon at their prayers, and the garlands are fixed up in the church, and make a tearing show. It is, however, unfortunate for the parish that the Wakes happen in the midst of the harvest, when they ought to be all at work, instead of amusing themselves with Races, Riot, and Drunkenness." *

In Derbyshire the rush-bearing clung to the villages in the High Peak till a late period, but, as far back as 1829, the custom had considerably declined, owing to new churches having been erected, and modern conveniences introduced. It has now entirely ceased. Mr. Farey, speaking of the rush-bearing at Chapel-en-le-Frith, states that it usually took place at the latter end of August, on public notice being given by the churchwardens of the rushes being mown and properly dried, in some marshy part of the parish, where the young people assemble. The carts are loaded with rushes, and decorated with flowers and ribands, and are attended to the church by the populace, many huzzaing and cracking whips by the side of the rush-cart, on their way thither, where everyone lends a hand in carrying in and spreading the rushes. At Whitwell, instead of rushes, the hay of a piece of grass-land, called the "church close," is annually, on Midsummer Eve, carted and spread in the church. †

Dr. Johnson has preserved an account of a pageant exhibited at Dent, in Yorkshire, on the rush-bearing (St. Bartholomew's Day), after the Restoration, in which, among other characters, "Oliver and Bradshaw, Rebellion and War, were represented, all decked by times with vizardes on, and strange deformities; and Bradshaw had his tongue run through with a red-hot iron, and Rebellion was hanged on a gibbet in the market-place. Then came Peace and Plenty, and

* Earwaker's "History of East Cheshire," 1877, vol. i., note, p. 81.
† Glover's "History of Derbyshire," 1829, vol. i., pp. 305-6.

UPPERMILL RUSHCART
(SIDE)

Diana with her nymphs, all with coronets on their heads, each of which made a several speech in verses of their loyalty to their king."

There are many quiet little valleys running into the hills on the east and south-east border of Lancashire, where the inhabitants retained many of their old manners and customs till a recent date, but the spread of manufacturing industry into these out-of-the-way places, and the introduction of railways, have led to a rapid increase in the population, and consequent change in its character. The parish of Saddleworth is a typical specimen, and bears the curious anomaly of being included in the County of York for civil, and in the diocese of Chester for ecclesiastical, purposes, a state of affairs which has given rise to a saying that, while York holds its body fast, Chester ministers to its soul. Comprising several hamlets, the rush-bearing (which takes place on the second Saturday after the 12th August), led to many rush-carts being drawn to the parish church at Saddleworth. Mr. George Shaw, J.P., who gave a lecture on the subject of rush-bearing in the Mechanics' Hall, Uppermill, on the 31st December, 1870,[*] states that at that time there were seldom more than two or three, though, in his early days, five or six, and on great occasions, such as election times, double that number appeared ; and that he once saw twelve at the church at one time. There are people yet living who remember as many as eight being drawn to the church on the Wakes Saturday. The last time rushes were spread in the church was in 1821 ; they were often spread to a depth of twelve to fifteen inches. After the rushes ceased to be used on the church floor, they were used as bedding for cattle. Some few years ago the landlord of the "Church Inn" used to give a sovereign a load for them, but of late years no cart has been taken up to the church.

[*] Reprinted in Bradbury's "Saddleworth Sketches," 1871, 8vo., pp. 253-259.

On ordinary occasions the rush-carts came from Cross, Boarshurst, Friezland, Running Hill, Harrop Dale, Burnedge, Uppermill, and Greenfield. "The Cross rush-cart always claimed precedence, and was allowed the privilege of backing up to the old porch of the church; the Boarshurst between the gate piers opposite, front to front; the Running Hill was generally stationed under the great yew tree; and the Friezland always went up to the 'Cross Keys Inn.' There seemed to be some tacit understanding that this should be the arrangement. How or why, I cannot tell, but I very well know that fifty years ago any other positions would have been deemed wrong, and entirely out of order."*

There is a tale told of Burnedge that, on a particularly wet wakes, they built their cart in a barn, but forgot the height of the barn door, and, when all was ready, it was discovered that it was higher than the doors, and it had to be partly pulled down, and, in this degraded state, dragged to the church, the builders consoling themselves with what is now an old adage, " If we cannot bring th' rush-cart to our minds, we must bring our minds to th' rush-cart."†

There is in the possession of Mr. Thomas Shaw, of St. Chad's, Uppermill, a very fine picture of Saddleworth rush-bearing in the olden time, but, unfortunately, both the name of the painter, and the date when it was executed, are unknown. It was painted from sketches made by his brother, Mr. George Shaw, and was probably executed about 1830, as the old church was pulled down in that year. In the centre of the picture is the old church of St. Chad, backed by the green hills, and flanked by the old yew, and an ash tree. Four rush-carts are represented in different positions, and the foreground is completely covered with a multi-

* "Saddleworth Sketches," p. 254.
† "Ibid."

UPPERMILL RUSHCART.
(BACK.)

tude of figures and booths. All the humours of such a scene are represented; the morris-dancers caper on the left hand; barrels of beer are being emptied by thirsty souls; and a donkey creates confusion in one corner by running away, upsetting everything in its way.

During the last fifteen years, there have been seven rush-carts built in Saddleworth, and the accompanying illustrations * will show how little variation in size and shape takes place.

Uppermill now takes the lead in the celebration of the wakes, known as "Longwood Thump." Last year (1889), the rush-cart was so badly made that the top fell to pieces, bringing down the riders. A row ensued, and in the *melée* the cart itself was broken. So disgraceful were some of the scenes witnessed in the evening, that many people thought no rush-cart would be made this year; but the landlord of the "Commercial Inn," being a new one, and wishing to ingratiate himself with his customers, called to his aid a number of men who were anxious to wipe out the failure of the previous year, and it was determined to have a rush-cart in the old style. A committee of twelve was appointed to superintend the affair. Subscriptions were canvassed for, a shilling constituting a member, and the rush-cart builder, now a sailor by profession, and who is considered the best builder of a rush-cart in the neighbourhood, set to work. Early on Sunday, the 17th August, a number of men went up the hill to the moss reserves to cut the long rushes needed for making the bolts, which must be of a superior kind to the short hard ones used for the body of the cart; and these rushes require to be selected as long as possible, and cut with a knife. In doing this, all the party got over knee-deep in the bog, some of

* The plates show the Uppermill rush-carts of 1875, 1880, 1881, 1888, 1889, and 1890; and the Greenfield rush-cart of 1888.

them up to their thighs, whilst one sank up to his waist, and had to be hauled out. They brought down fifteen large bundles of fine, pliant rushes, none less than four feet six inches, and many over six feet in length. On the Monday, the builder of the rush-cart proceeded to tie them up into bolts four inches in diameter, rejecting all the broken ones. An assistant, in the meantime, mowed the shorter rushes required for the body of the cart, and brought them in to be tied up in larger bundles ready for the building. It was at first intended to build the cart in a small field behind the inn, but, on sinking holes for the wheels, the ground was found to be so soddened with the late heavy rains, that it was considered unsafe to trust so great a weight as the rush-cart on it, and it had, therefore, to be made in the yard, where the ground was firmer. The cart was one of the small two-wheeled ones used for carting stone in the neighbourhood, and was sunk in the ground up to the axle, being further secured by slotches, and trestles under the shafts, so as to render it immovable. At noon, on Thursday, the actual building of the cart began. An iron rod, bent to the angle required, was fixed at each corner, and tied at the top, to strengthen the structure and guide the builder in placing the rushes. The body of the cart, having been filled with loose rushes, well trodden down, the bundles—the ends cut straight with a scythe blade—were laid, keeping the face as nearly as possible to the curves it would finally assume, the longer and finer bolts being placed with the ends to the front and back of the cart only, and not transversely as well, as in the carts made in some places. Being twice the usual diameter also, they gave the edge a more substantial, but less pleasing, appearance, and, in addition, did not project so much as usual, being only six inches at the bottom, and increasing to twelve inches at the top of the cart; yet they were

UPPERMILL RUSHCART.
(FRONT.)

further kept in position by having a strip of long, narrow white lath up each side. When the bundles in the body of the cart were laid in their places, the string that bound them was cut, so that the rushes might lay closely together, and were well pressed down, so as to make the whole structure as substantial and compact as possible. The usual height to which the rushes are piled in these small carts is from nine to ten feet above the side, but, as the maker was determined to make a finer and better one than that of last year, he decided to build twelve feet. This required great care in consolidating the rushes and keeping to the curves, any deviation from which would have entailed a similar disaster to last year. This great height, for so small a base (six feet by four feet), as will be noticed on looking at the illustrations, gives the rush-cart a very tall appearance, much different to the huge, substantial ones which used to be built in waggons, and which, to the same height, were half as much longer and wider. This peculiarity is to be observed in all the rush-carts built in the hill districts, in former times as well as the present. Having arrived at a height of ten feet, the builder began to use the bolts made of long rushes, in order to bind the top together as much as possible, and, finally, as these left a small face unfilled along the top, made two good bundles of rushes, which were placed across the others, or lengthways, to fill up this space, and afford a more comfortable seat for the two men who had to ride upon it. The sides swelled out (at the cart wheel) to a distance of eighteen inches, and then gradually sloped upwards and inwards to the the top, the greatest projection being at a height of two feet six inches above the side of the cart. The front and back did not curve outwards, but sloped gradually inwards from bottom to top.

The builder and his assistants had proceeded so far

by Friday night, but a strong, south-westerly gale springing up in the night-time, accompanied by torrents of rain, daylight on Saturday revealed a most unpleasant state of affairs, for, as the cart was being built in a yard sheltered on two sides by high buildings, it had not been thought necessary to secure the top with ropes, and the settling down of the rushes, caused by the rain which soaked in, and the strain of the wind on so high and narrow a structure, had bent over the cart to one side, the mischief being aided by the sinking of one of the wheels. Though somewhat disheartened, the builders commenced to put the best face upon the matter that could be done, for to have had no rush-cart after the trouble that had been taken, and the boasting which had taken place, would never do. To take down the rushes in order to straighten it would be to nearly dismantle the cart, and time was pressing, so it was decided to get boards and ropes, and endeavour to pull the top over into something like its original shape, and then trust to the man who pares the faces of the cart to put as presentable an appearance as possible upon it. This was done, and though several inches were pared off one side, yet it left the cart with a most unpleasant-looking hoist. The substantial character of the building was, however, shown by the treatment it received, and survived. This led to a delay of a couple of hours, and as it had been stated that the rush-cart would be drawn out about three o'clock, and as much remained to be done, every hand that could be found room for was set to work. Trestles were placed, and whilst one man pared the face of the rushes smooth and into shape with a scythe blade, others were making fresh blades as sharp as a razor, for the toughness and density of the rushes took the edge off the blades very quickly. This paring is rather a dangerous business, for, the blade slipping, the man nearly cut off his thumb, and, two years ago, a man almost cut his left hand off.

UPPERMILL RUSHCART.
(THREE QUARTER.)

Others procured two large branches of ash, and tying them securely to strong pointed stakes, drove them down into the rushes at the top of the cart, leaving the centre clear for the riders. Another was trimming the edges, or "feathering," with a pair of shears, whilst the front of the cart was being embellished with the sheet. This was a piece of bleached calico, cut to the shape of the front of the cart, and was ornamented with a border of red and blue braid, crossed diagonally, and in the diamonds thus formed were fastened artificial flowers. At the bottom of the sheet was a large rosette of silver and gold tinsel and blue ribbon, above which was a large crown in silver. This was surmounted by the figures "1890," in white, on a black ground. Then came a large heart in silver, on which was displayed some coloured scraps, artificial flowers, of various kinds and colours, filled up the blank spaces, and the whole affair, when the sun shone upon it, had a most gorgeous appearance. No plate has been displayed on the Saddleworth rush-carts for some years past. Natural flowers were stuck in the ends of the bolts, both at the front and back of the cart. These were to have been dahlias of various colours, a number of which had been promised, but, failing to arrive, resource was had to the neighbouring gardens, and shift made with such flowers as they afforded. New ropes were attached to the ends of the shafts, the latter being crossed by a number of strong wooden bars, to enable the men to hold up the front of the cart, and check its descent down hill. In these ropes "stretchers," seven feet wide, were placed, the first at a distance of ten feet from the shafts, the remainder (of which there were six) at intervals of six feet.

As the moment for drawing-out arrived, the excitement became intense; the inn-yard was crammed with men and boys all wanting to have a hand in hauling in the ropes. Trestles and props were knocked away, the

ground in front of the wheels dug out, the ropes run
out to their full length, and the stretchers manned by
as many as could lay hold (I counted over seventy
drawers), who roughly sized themselves, the boys next
the cart, increasing in height to the tallest in front.
Two men mounted the cart, sitting back to back, and
steadied themselves by the large branches before-
mentioned. This post is one much coveted, although
rather dangerous. I have been informed of three men
who have fallen off and broken their backs, and have
myself witnessed several ugly falls, but these chiefly
occur through the rider getting too much beer. In the
present instance one of the riders had provided himself
with a tin can tied to the end of a long string, so as
not to miss his share through inability to reach it.
The whip was now brought out, it was twelve feet
long, having a lash two feet long at the end, and was
an inch and a quarter thick at the handle. It had been
well oiled several times in order to make it pliable,
and was a most formidable implement. The "band"
now collected, consisting of two fifers and a drummer,
and, everything being ready, the men laid hold of the
shafts, the boys began "girding," or straining at the
ropes, the word "neaw lads" was given, and for a
moment quietness reigned, but the music struck up,
the men shouted, the cart gave a slight heave, and then
rose up to the level ground as the strain told. Till
now there had been but little noise, but as soon as the
cart began to move freely a most extraordinary sight
presented itself, for the music changing to the old rush-
cart tune, a cheer was given, and instantly the whole
of the drawers commenced to dance, if such it may be
termed, or rather capered most vigorously, at the same
time swaying from side to side of the road, and carrying the stretchers high above their heads. The cart
was now run into the square, where it was greeted with
a cheer from the crowd assembled to witness the

UPPERMILL BRASS-BAND, 1890.

spectacle. Here a rest was taken, beer served round, and the cart and its ornaments criticised by the onlookers.

The scene which presented itself was an extremely picturesque one. On one side of the square runs the high road, lined on one side with stalls and booths of various descriptions, containing nuts, gingerbread, hot-peas, toys, and pots. The square itself was filled with other stalls of a similar character, swing-boats, and a merry-go-round, whilst the whole was backed by the clean-looking grey stone houses, above which towered a couple of factory chimneys, the blue hills in the distance just giving it a rural look, and leading the mind to the quieter scenes beyond.[*]

Having refreshed themselves, and decided on the route to be taken, the carter cracked his whip, the band struck up "The girl I left behind me," the drawers began capering, and, with a shout, the rush-cart started on its way to Greenfield, calling at all the public-houses on the way, where the drawers were liberally regaled with ale, and contributions given to the expenses of the show.

The illustrations of the cart here given[+] show it when the building was completed, and before the sides had been pared to their proper shape and smooth surface. They also show the damage done by the storm, and, notwithstanding the care spent upon its building, the cart, which was to excel any previous one, was finally judged by its makers as "th' worst we ever made." It cost just £9 in building, of which the builder had £1 for his services, and weighed about fifty cwt. On the Tuesday, the rushes were given to the owner of the cart, as some recompense for the damage done to it last year.

[*] See Frontispiece.
[+] See Uppermill Rush-cart—side, back, front, and three-quarter.

Garlands in Churches.

T was customary to decorate the churches for the greater festivals and special occasions from a very early period:

"1602. Paid for Flowers and Rushes for the church when the Queene was in town - - - xxd."
—*Churchwardens' Accounts, St. Lawrence, Reading.*

The old rushes were removed, the floor and walls swept, and the church "dressed" for the ceremony. This consisted of garlands and flowers, which were often put in their places before the rushes were brought in; but, on the other hand, the garlands used in the procession were deposited after the rushes were laid. The Churchwardens' Accounts, Wilmslow, Cheshire, contain several payments for this service:

"1618. Paid for dressinge of ye church - - xxd.
1621. Paid for dressinge the church against the Rush-bearinge - - - - ijs.
1631. Paid for dressing the church at the Rush-bearing - - - - - ijs."

Garlands of natural flowers were extensively used, and were often gathered at the expense of the parish:

"1626. Payde for dressinge the greate Churche Garlande, which wee gathered in Bollen ffee - - - - - iiijs. vjd."
—*Churchwardens' Accounts, Wilmslow.*

"1796. Pd. Mary Burrowes for Dressing Singers' Garland - - - - - - - 2s."
Churchwardens' Accounts, Holmes Chapel.

Lysons * states that the rush-bearing " was attended by a procession of young men and women, dressed in ribbands, and carrying garlands, etc., which were hung up in the church. We saw these garlands remaining in several places."

Finney, who wrote a MS. "History of Wilmslow," speaks of the garlands of tinsel and paper hung up in the church. Those borne at the rush-bearing were also placed there, "and make a tearing show."

Bagshaw † says Astbury Church "was once adorned with garlands and flowers, and the seats and floor covered with rushes; but this custom has fallen into disuse."

The "Bristol Times and Mirror," 2nd June, 1879, contains an account of the "Rush Sunday at St. Mary Redcliff Church," which is interesting :

"Yesterday, being Whit-Sunday, the ancient custom of strewing the floors of St. Mary Redcliff Church with rushes was observed, and the Mayor, with a large number of the members of the Corporation, attended the morning service. The magnificent parish church had been decorated for the occasion. Azaleas, rhododendrons, water-lilies, etc., were arranged on each side of the altar, and the effect enhanced by the blending of the colours was extremely pleasing. On the altar were crosses, composed of the finest white and red azaleas, etc., with beds of mosses and floral devices. The top rails of the front choir-stalls were lined with strings of blue-bells, lilies, white azaleas, and evergreens, and in front of the reading-desk was a sacred monogram, worked in somewhat similar flowers, while the panels and base were also decorated. The decorations of the pulpit were not so extensive, but were chaste. Special pains had been expended upon the font, which was surmounted by a floral canopy, the base being divided into panels by strings of flowers, in the centre of which were various devices, embedded in moss and evergreens. Crowds assembled in front of the Council-house and around the church to view the starting and arrival of the civic procession, the pageant apparently lacking none of its old attractions. Admission was by ticket until the arrival of the Mayor and Corporation, when the doors were thrown open, and the sacred edifice was soon filled to overflowing. The sermon was preached by Canon Norris, B.D., Vicar of the parish."

       * "Magna Britannia," Cheshire, 1810, p. 463.
       † "History of Cheshire," 1850, p. 412.

A description of the quaint custom at Castleton, in Derbyshire, will form a fitting sequel to the foregoing. It has long been the custom here to make a huge garland of flowers on the 29th May, heading a procession formed of the villagers, which parades the streets. I saw this garland made on the 29th May, 1885. The framework was of wood, thatched with straw. Interior diameter, a little over two feet, outside (when covered with flowers), over three feet six inches. In shape it

CASTLETON GARLAND.

somewhat resembled a bell, completely covered over with wild flowers—hyacinths, water-buttercups, buttercups, daisies, forget-me-nots, wallflowers, rhododendrons, tulips, and ornamental grasses, in rows, each composed of the same flower, which had been gathered in the neighbourhood the evening before. The top, called the "queen," was formed of garden flowers, and fits into a socket at the top of the garland. It weighed over a hundredweight, required two men to lift it, and had occupied four men from noon till five o'clock in the afternoon to make. This garland is borne on the head and shoulders of a man riding a horse, and wearing a red jacket. A stout handle inside, which rests on the saddle in front of him, enables him to hold it upright. It completely envelopes him to the waist, and is roomy enough to enable ale to be passed up to his mouth, of which he took good care to have a share. His horse is led for him, preceded by a band of music, and followed by another man on horseback, dressed as a woman, who acts the fool. These are followed by the villagers, dancing, even old people who can scarcely walk making a point of attempting to dance on this, the greatest day in the year at Castleton. After parading the village, the "queen" is taken off the garland and placed in the church, the garland being hoisted with ropes to the top of the church tower, where it is placed on one of the pinnacles and left till it has withered away, when the framework is taken down and kept for another year. The other pinnacles have branches of oak.

The procession starts at six o'clock in the evening from the inn whose turn it is to take the lead in the festivities, as the villagers have their work to attend to during the day. The country people flock from all parts; but the custom, fortunately, is not sufficiently known to ensure the attendance of the riff-raff from the towns, whose presence would soon vitiate its primitive simplicity, and sow the seeds of its decay.

Garlands were formerly placed on the top of the tower of Whalley Church, Lancashire. At Didsbury, and at Eccles also, garlands were formerly suspended in the churches. Dr. Wray, one of the vicars of Rochdale, made an order that, " the garlands should not be suffered to stay in the church after Monday. In the year 1770, numbers of women were seen returning home in liquor at six o'clock on Tuesday morning.

The old custom of bringing the garlands on the Saturday, and fetching them on the Monday from the church, where they are deposited on the Saturday evening, may be continued."

At Droylsden, near Manchester, the garland, which always preceded the rush-cart, was placed in the chapel at Newton Heath. Four beams projected between the windows on the north side, one of which appertained to each township, for the purpose of displaying, for four years, the garland which had preceded its rush-bearing. The garland consisted of a wooden framework, several yards in circumference, ornamented with artificial flowerets, cut in divers-coloured papers, and surmounted with a tinsel crown or the imitation of a bird, conventionally treated. Each township, as its turn came round, every fourth year, fetched out its old garland, and, by dint of reconstruction and improvement, attempted to surpass all previous efforts of the rival villages. *

A writer in Hone's "Year Book," 1831, speaking of Grasmere Church, says that he was "particularly attracted by the paper garlands which he found deposited in the vestry. They were curiously and tastefully cut, and he was almost tempted to beg one."

* Higson's "History of Droylsden," 1859, p. 65.

THE MORRIS-DANCERS.

The Morris-Dancers.

THE morris-dance was introduced into England from Spain in the sixteenth century, and speedily became popular, so much so, that it was engrafted on a more ancient pageant, that of the play of Robin Hood, and the characters partook of both. "The morris-dance, in which bells are gingled," says Dr. Johnson, "or staves or swords clashed, was learned by the Moors, and was probably a kind of Pyerhic or military dance." "Morisco," says Blount, "(Span.) a Moor; also a Dance, so called, wherein there were usually five men, and a boy dressed in a girle's habit, whom they called the Maid Marrion, or perhaps Morian, from the Italian Morione, a headpiece, because her head was wont to be gaily trimmed up. Common people call it a Morris-Dance." It is supposed that its name, in Spanish *Morisco*, a Moor, points to its origin; and it was popular in France as early as the fifteenth century, under the name of *Morisque*. It was probably introduced into this country by dancers both from Spain and France, for in the earlier English allusions to it it is sometimes called the *Morisco*, and sometimes the *Morisce* or *Morisk*. Douce says it has been supposed to have been first brought into England in the time of Edward III., "when John of Gaunt returned from Spain,[†] but it is much more probable that we had it

---

[*] "Glossographia," 1656.
[†] See Peck's "Memoirs of Milton," p. 135.

from our Gallic neighbours, or even from the Flemings."

At a splendid feast given by Gaston de Foix, at Vendome, in 1458, "foure young laddes and a damosell, attired like savages, daunced (by good direction) an excellent *Morisco*, before the assembly."* Coquillart,† a French poet, who wrote about 1470, says that the Swiss danced the Morisco to the beat of the drum. Tabourot (Thoinot Arbeau)‡ relates that in his youthful days it was the custom in good societies for a boy to come into the hall, when supper was finished, with his face blackened, his forehead bound with white or yellow taffeta, and bells tied to his legs. He then proceeded to dance the *Morisco*, the whole length of the hall, backwards and forwards, to the great amusement of the company. He hints that the bells might have been borrowed from the *crotali* of the ancients in the Pyrrhic dance. He then describes the more modern morris-dance, which was performed by striking the ground with the forepart of the feet; but, as this was found to be too fatiguing, the motion was afterwards confined to the heel, the toes being kept firm, by which means the dancer contrived to rattle his bells with more effect. He adds that this mode of dancing fell into disuse, as it was found to bring on gouty complaints. This is the air to which the last-mentioned morris was performed:

* Favine's "Theater of Honour," p. 345.
† "Œuvres," p. 127.
‡ "Orchesographie," etc., 1589, 46.

One of the accounts of Petrarch's coronation says that after supper, to amuse the company, composed of the most handsome Roman ladies, he danced "en pourpoint une belle et vigoreuse *moresque*," with little bells attached to his arms and legs, an act which they regarded as a token of politeness and greatness of mind, worthy of a poet who had just triumphed.*

Douce says it appears that the *Morisco*, or Moor dance, is exceedingly different from the morris-dance formerly practised in this country, it being performed with the castanets or rattles, at the ends of the fingers, and not with bells attached to various parts of the dress. The real and uncorrupted Moorish dance was to be found in Spain, where it still continues to delight both natives and strangers under the name of the *fandango*. It may be likewise remarked that the exquisitely pretty music to this lively dance is undoubtedly Moorish.†

At a religious ceremony in Spain, exhibited on Corpus Christi Day, James I.'s ambassador, the Earl of Nottingham, attended, and a spectator records that there were among the parties to it eight giants, and two Moors with tabor and pipe playing, and he was scandalised by observing that "the dragons, giants, and morrice-dancers paraded and danced in the very ranks of the friars' procession."‡

The earliest representation of the morris-dance is an exceedingly scarce engraving on copper by Israel Van Mecheln, or Meckenen, so named from the place of his nativity, a German village on the confines of Flanders, in which latter country this artist appears chiefly to have resided, and therefore in most of his prints we may observe the Flemish costume of his time. From the pointed shoes that we see in one of the figures, it must have been executed between the years 1460 and 1470, about which latter period the broad-

* "Mem. de Petrarque," ii., append. 3, 9.
† "Illustrations of Shakspeare," etc., 1839, pp. 577-578.
‡ "Somers Tracts."

MORRIS-DANCERS, c. 1470.
From a print by Israel van Mecheln.

MUNICH MORRIS-DANCERS, c. 1480 (Figs. 4, 5, and 6).

MUNICH MORRIS-DANCERS, C. 1480 (Figs. 7, 8, 9, and 10).

toed shoes came into fashion in France and Flanders.
It seems to have been intended as a pattern for gold-
smiths' work, probably a cup or tankard. The artist,
in a fancy representation of foliage, has introduced
several figures belonging to a Flemish May-game
morris, consisting of the lady of the May, the fool, the
piper, two morris-dancers with bells and streamers, and
four other dancing characters, for which appropriate
names will not easily be found.*

In the old town-hall at Munich there is a series of
ten figures of morris-dancers, carved in wood by
Erasmus Schnitznar, in 1480, and described by Helen
Zimmern in the "Art Journal."† They are in niches
in the frieze of the State Room (called the "dancing
room"), and formerly consisted of twelve figures, but
two were given by Louis I. of Bavaria to the sculptor
Schwanthaler, who discovered them, and caused them
to be cleaned. All the figures have bells, and No. 6
has the long streamers to his sleeves. The Moor is
represented by figure 4.

At Betley, in Staffordshire, there is a painted
window representing a set of morris-dancers, which is
described in Steeven's "Shakspeare" (Henry IV., part
1). There are eleven figures and a maypole: 1. Robin
Hood; 2. Maid Marian; 3. Friar Tuck: 4, 6, 7, 10,
and 11. Morris-dancers; 5. The hobby-horse; 8. The
maypole; 9. The piper; and 12. The fool. Figures 10
and 11 have long streamers to the sleeves, and all the
dancers have bells, either at the ankles, wrists, or knees.
There is a striking resemblance between these figures
and those in Israel's engraving, and it would seem that
the period of execution, as to both, was nearly the
same. Tollet, the owner of the window, thought it
was of the time of Henry VIII., c. 1535, but Douce
attributes it to that of Edward IV., which appears more

* Douce, "Illustrations of Shakspeare," etc., p. 685.
† 1885, pp. 121-124.

MORRIS-DANCERS, C. 1500.
From a painted window at Betley.

likely to be the case.* The figures of the English
friar, maypole, and hobby-horse seem to be an addition
of later date.

Walpole, in his "Catalogue of English Engravers,"
under the name of Peter Stent, describes a painting at
Lord Fitzwilliam's, on Richmond Green, which came
out of the old neighbouring palace. It was executed by
Vinckenboom, about the end of the reign of James I.,
and exhibits a view of the above palace. A morris-
dance is introduced, consisting of seven figures, viz. :
a fool, hobby-horse, piper, Maid Marian, and three
dancers, the rest of the figures being spectators. Of
these, the first four and one of the dancers Douce has
reduced in a plate from a tracing made by Grose.
The fool has an inflated bladder, or eel-skin, with a
ladle at the end of it, and with this he is collecting money.
The piper is pretty much in his original state; but the
hobby-horse wants the legerdemain apparatus, and Maid
Marian is not remarkable for the elegance of her person.

Few, if any, vestiges of the morris-dance can be
traced in England beyond the reign of Henry VII.,
about which time, and particularly in that of Henry
VIII., the churchwardens' accounts in several parishes
afford materials that throw much light on the subject,
and show that the morris-dance made a very considerable figure in the parochial festivals.

The Churchwardens' Accounts of Kingston-upon-
Thames, contain numerous entries relating to Robin
Hood and the morris-dancers, as :

"1508. For paynting of the *Mores* garments, and
   for sarten gret leveres - - - 0 2 4
 ,, For plyts and ½ of laun for the *Mores*
   garments - - - - - - 0 2 11

* This window was first engraved in Johnson and Steeven's "Shakspeare,"
1778, 8vo., at the end of the first part of Henry IV.; in Reed's, and also Malone's
editions; in Gutch's "Lytell Geste of Robin Hode," 1847, appendix, p. 349; and
in Brand's "Popular Antiquities," 1879, 8vo., Chatto & Windus. There is a
large coloured plate of it in Sangster's re-issue of Knight's "Old England, or the
Museum of Antiquities."

MORRIS-DANCERS, temp. JAMES I.
From a painting by Vinchenboom.

"1508.   For Orseden for the same   0   0 10
   ,,   For bellys for the daunsars   0   0 12
1509-10. For silver paper for the *Mores*-dawnsars   0   0   7
1519-20. Shoes for the *Mores*-daunsars, the frere,
             and Mayde Maryan, at 7d. a peyre   0   5   4
1521-22. Eight yerds of fustyan for the *Mores*-
             daunsars' coats   0 16   0
   ,,   A dosyn of gold skynnes for the Morres   0   0 10
1536-37. Five hats and 4 porses for the daunsars   0   0   4½."

In 1536-37, amongst other clothes belonging to the actors in the play of Robin Hood, left in the keeping of the churchwardens were: "4 *Morres-daunsars* cotes of white fustian spangelyd, and two gryne saten cotes, and a dysard's [fool's] cote of cotton, and 6 payre of garters with bells." In 1537-38, the articles comprised: "a Mouren's [Moor's] cote of buckram, and four morres-daunsars' cotes of white fustian spangelid, and two gryne saten cotes, and disardde's cote of cotton, and six payre of garters with belles."

In Coates' "History of Reading," the churchwardens' accounts of St. Mary's parish are said to contain the following entries:

"1557. Item, payed to the Morrys-Daunsars and
           the Mynstrelles, mete and drink at
           Whitsontide   0   3   4
       Payed to them the Sonday after May Day   0   0 20
       Pd. to the Painter for painting of their
           cotes   0   2   8
       Pd. to the Painter for 2 doz. of Lyvereys   0   0 20."

The following curious notice is taken from the original accounts of St. Giles', Cripplegate, 1571, preserved in MS. Addit. 12,222, f. 5:

"Item, paide in charges by the appointment of the parishioners, for the settinge forth of a gyaunt morres-dainsers, with vj. calyvers and iij boies on horsback, to go in the watche befoore the Lorde Maiore uppon Midsomer even, as may appere by particulers for the furnishinge of the same, vj.li., ixs., ixd."

It appears from the Churchwardens' Accounts of Great Marlow that dresses for the morris-dance "were lent out to the neighbouring parishes. They are accounted for so late as 1629."*

In 1557, there was a May-game in Fenchurch Street, London, with a Lord and Lady of the May, and a *morris-dance*.†

The allusions to the morris-dancers became very frequent in writers of the time of Queen Elizabeth. In a rare tract of this period, entitled "Plaine Perceval, the Peace-Maker of England," mention is made of a "stranger, which seeing a quintessence (beside the Foole and the Maid Marian) of all the picked youth, strained out of a whole endship, footing the Morris about a May-pole, and he, not hearing the minstrelsie for the fidling, the tune for the sound, nor the pipe for the noise of the tabor, bluntly demaunded if they were not all beside themselves, that they so lip'd and skip'd without an occasion."‡

Shakspeare, in "Henry V.," mentions the Whitsun morris-dance :

"And let us do it with no show of fear ;
No ! with no more than if we heard that England
Were busied with a Whitsun morris-dance."

And in another play, "All's Well that Ends Well," act ii., sc. 2, he speaks of the fitness of a "morris for May-day." In later times the morris was frequently introduced upon the stage. Stephen Gosson, who wrote about 1579, in a little tract entitled "Players Confuted," speaks of "dauncing of gigges, galiardes, and *morices*, with hobbi-horses," as stage performances.

Herrick, in his "Hesperides," speaking of country blessings, says among them were :

"Thy *Wakes*, thy Quintals, here thou hast,
Thy Maypoles, too, with garlands grac't ;
Thy *Morris-dance ;* thy Whitsun ale ;
Thy Sheering flat, which never fail."

* Langley's "Antiquities of Desborough," 1797, 4to., p. 142.
† Strypes' "Eccl. Memorials," iii., p. 376.
‡ Brand's "Observations on Popular Antiquities."

A KNIGHT ERRANT.

THE MORRIS-DANCERS.

In Laneham's letter from Kenilworth Castle, a Bride Ale is described, in which mention is made of "a lively Moris-dauns, according to the Auncient manner: six dauncerz, Mawdmarion, and the fool."

To the puritans, the morris-dance was particularly obnoxious, and their diatribes against it are numerous and severe. Stubbes, in his "Anatomie of Abuses," 1585, p. 107, describes it as follows: "They strike up the *Devil's Daunce* withall, then marcht this heathen company towards the church and churchyarde, their pypers pyping, their drummers thundering, their stumpes dauncing, their belles ingling, their handkerchiefes fluttering about their heades like madde men, their hobbie-horses and other monsters skirmishing amongst the throng; and in this sorte they go to the church (though the minister be at prayer or preaching), dauncing and swinging their handkerchiefes over their heades in the church, like Devils incarnate, with such a confused noise that no man can heare his own voyce." Another of these credulous fanatics[*] writes: "The second abuse, which of all others is the greatest, is this, that it hath been toulde that your dauncers have daunced naked in nettes."

Richard Baxter, who was more moderate in his opinions, and his testimony, therefore, of greater value, in his "Divine Appointment of the Lord's Day," tells us: "I have lived in my youth in many places where sometimes shows or uncouth spectacles have been their sports at certain seasons of the year, and sometimes *morrice-dancings*, and sometimes stage plays, and sometimes *wakes* and revels. . . . And when the people by the book [of Sports] were allowed to play and dance out of public service-time, they could so hardly break off their sports that many a time the reader was fain to stay till the piper and players would give over; and

[*] Fetherston's "Dialogue agaynst light, lewde, and lascivious dauncing," 1582, 12mo., sign D 7. See a passage to the same purpose in Northbrooke's "Treatise against dicing, dauncing, etc.," 1597, 4to., fo. 68 *b*.

sometimes the *morrice-dancers* would come into the church in all the linen, and scarfs, and antic dresses, with morrice-bells jingling at their legs. And as soon as common-prayer was read did haste out presently to their play again."

In Ben Jonson's play of "Bartholomew Fair" (1614), a puritan, who was once a baker, but now dreams and sees visions, "gave over his trade, out of a scruple he took that in spiced conscience, those cakes he made were served to bridals, maypoles, *morrices*, and such profane feasts and meetings;" and he describes "stage-players, rhymers, and *morrice-dancers*," as a beam in the eye of the brethren.

Barnaby Rich, also,† has a fling at the extravagance of dress in 1615: "And from whence commeth this wearing, and this embroidery of long locks, this curiosity that is used amongst men, in frizeling and curling of their haire, this gentlewoman-like starcht bands, so be-edged and belaced, fitter for Maid Marion in a Moris-dance then for him that hath either that spirit or courage that should be in a gentleman?"

Notwithstanding these objectors, the morris-dance remained as popular as ever, and Thomas Hall, in his "Funebriæ Floræ, the downe fall of May-games," (1660), 4to., observes: "If Moses were angry when he saw the people dance about a golden calf, well may we be angry to see people *dancing the morrice* about a post in honour of a whore, as you shall see anon."

The following description of a morris-dance occurs in "Cobbe's Prophecies, his Signes, and Tokens, his Madrigalls, Questions, and Answers" (1614):

> "It was my hap of late, by chance,
> To meet a Country Morris dance,
> When, cheefest of them all, the Foole
> Plaied with a ladle and a toole;
> When every younger shak't his bells
> Till sweating feet gave fohing smells;

† "The honestie of this age." 4to., p. 35.

> "And fine Maide Marian, with her smoile,
> Shew'd how a rascall plaied the voile;
> But, when the Hobby-horse did wihy,
> Then all the wenches gave a tihy;
> But when they gan to shake their boxe,
> And not a goose could catch a foxe,
> The piper then put up his pipes,
> And all the woodcocks look't like snipes," etc.

A morris-dance in Fleet Street, London, is described in a seventeenth century manuscript in the Harleian M.S., 3910:

> "In Fleet strete then I heard a shoote;
> I putt of my hatt, and I made no staye,
> And when I came unto the rowte,
> Good Lord! I heard a taber playe,
> For so, God save mee! a *morrys-daunce*.
> Oh ther was sport alone for mee
> To see the hobby-horse how he did praunce
> Among the gingling company,
> I proffer'd them money for their coats,
> But my conscience had remorse,
> For my father had no oates,
> And I must have had the hobbie-horse."

King James I. in his Declaration, 24th May, 1618, orders that the people should not be debarred from "having of May-games, Whitson-ales, and *Morris-dances*, and the setting up of Maypoles."

Greene's "Quip for an Upstart Courtier" (1620) describes that effeminate youth as acting the part of Maid Marian: "to make the foole as faire, forsooth, as if he were to play Maid Marian in a May-game or a *Morris-Dance*."

In Pasquil's "Palinodia" (1634), we are told that:

> "The lords of castles, mannors, townes, and towers,
> Rejoic'd when they beheld the farmers flourish,
> And would come downe unto the summer-bowers,
> To see the country-gallants *dance the Morrice*."

Among the Crown jewels, on the accession of Charles I., there was "One Salte of goulde, called the *Morris-Daunce*." Its foot was garnished with six great sapphires, fifteen diamonds, thirty-seven rubies, and forty-two small pearls; upon the border, about the shank, twelve diamonds, eighteen rubies, and fifty-two pearls, and standing about that were *five Morris-daunccrs and Taberer*, having amongst them thirteen small garnishing pearls and one ruby. *The Lady* holding the salt had upon her garment, from her foot to her face, fifteen pearls and eighteen rubies. Upon the foot of the same salt were four coarse rubies and four coarse diamonds; upon the border, about the middle of the salt, were four coarse diamonds, seven rubies, and eight pearls; and upon the top of the said salt, four diamonds, four rubies, and three great pearls; [the lady] had upon the tyre of her head ten rubies, twelve diamonds, and twenty-nine garnishing pearls. By a special warrant of Charles I., dated at Hampton Court, 7th December, 1625, a large quantity of gold plate and jewels of great value were transferred to the Duke of Buckingham and the Earl of Holland, Ambassadors-Extraordinary to the United Provinces, who were thereby authorised to transport and dispose of them beyond the seas, in such manner as the king had previously directed these noblemen in private. The splendid gold salt called the *Morris-Dance*, above described, weighing one hundred and fifty-one ounces and three-quarters, was thus disposed of.*

On the first May-day after the restoration of Charles II. (in 1661), a maypole was erected in the Strand. In the procession which took place to it was "a *Morice-Dance*, finely deckt, with purple scarfs, in their half-shirts, with a Tabor and Pipe, the ancient Musick, and danced round about the Maypole, and after that danced the rounds of their liberty." † There is an engraving, by Vertue, of this procession, in the prints belonging to the Society of Antiquaries.

* Hone's "Year Book," 1832, p. 428.
† "Cities Loyalty Displayed," 1661, 4to.

In "Articles of Visitation and Inquiry for the Diocese of St. David" (1662) occurs the following: "Have no minstrels, no *morris-dancers*, no dogs, hawks, or hounds been suffered to be brought or come into your church, to the disturbance of the congregation?"

Other writers refer to the early morris-dance:

"The queen stood on some doubt of a Spanish invasion, though it proved but a *morris-dance* upon our waves." *Wotton.*

"How like an everlasting *morris-dance* it looks,
Nothing but hobby-horse and maid-marrian."
—*Massenger's Very Woman*, iii., 2.

"One, in his catalogue of a feigned library, sets down this title of a book, 'The *morris-dance* of hereticks.'" *Bacon.*

"The sounds and seas, with all their finny drove,
Now to the moon in wavering *morrice* move."
Milton.

"I took delight in pieces that shewed a country village, *morrice-dancing*, and peasants together by the ears." *Peacham.*

Mr. Waldron, the editor of "The Sad Shepherd" (1783, p. 255), mentions seeing a company of morris-dancers in the summer of 1783, at Richmond, Surrey, from Abingdon. They were accompanied by a fool, in a motley jacket, who carried in his hand a staff about two feet long, with a blown bladder at the end of it, with which he either buffeted the crowd to keep them at a proper distance from the dancers, or played tricks for the diversion of the spectators. The dancers and the fool were Berkshire husbandmen taking an annual circuit to collect money. Another company of this kind was seen at Usk, in Monmouthshire, which was attended by a boy Maid Marian, a hobby-horse, and a fool. They professed to have kept up the ceremony at that place for the last three hundred years.

The "Star," of the 9th August, 1792, states that, "On Monday [July 30th], the morris-dancers of Pendleton paid their annual visit in Salford. They were adorned with all the variety of colours that a profusion of ribbons could give them, and had a very showy garland."

Hone saw a troop of Hertfordshire morris-dancers performing in Goswell Road, London, in 1826; and a correspondent, writing to the "Every Day Book,"* describes what was evidently the same company as being in Rosoman Street, Clerkenwell, in June of the same year:

> "They consisted of eight young men, six of whom were dancers, the seventh played the pipe and tabor, and the eighth, the head of them, collected the pence in his hat, and put the precious metal into the slit of a tin painted box, under lock and key, suspended before him. The tune the little rural-noted pipe played to the gentle pulsations of the tabor, is called:
> 'Moll in the wad and I fell out,
> And what d'ye think it was about.'
> This may be remembered as one of the once popular street songs of the late Charles Dibdin's composition. The dancers wore party-coloured ribands round their hats, arms, and knees, to which a row of small latten bells were appended, somewhat like those which are given to amuse infants in teeth-cutting, that tinkled with the motion of the wearers. These rustic adventurers . . . came from a village in Hertfordshire. . . . The 'set to,' as they termed it, expressed a vis à vis address. They then turned, returned, clapped their hands before and behind, and made a jerk with the knee and foot alternately. . . . They intended sojourning in town a week or two, after which the box will be opened, and an equitable division take place, previously to the commencement of mowing and hay harvest. . . . It was the third year of their pilgrimage."

Gutch,† writing in 1847, says that a very few years before, he witnessed "a numerous retinue of morris-dancers, remarkably well habited, skilfully performing their evolutions to the tune of a tabor and pipe, in the streets of Oxford University; and he is credibly informed that at Chipping Norton and other towns in Oxfordshire a band of dancers traverse the neighbourhood for many days at Whitsuntide. At Droitwich, also, in Worcestershire, on the 27th of June, a large

---

* 1827, vol. 2, pp. 792-795.
† "Lytell Geste of Robin Hode," 1847, note, p. 365.

party of morris-dancers still continue to parade the town and neighbourhood, it is said, in commemoration of a discovery of some extensive salt mines."

Miss Baker, in her "Glossary of Northamptonshire Words" (1854), speaks of them as still met with in that county; and Halliwell [*] also speaks of the morris-dance as still commonly practised in Oxfordshire, though the old costume had been forgotten, and the performers were only dressed with a few ribbons. Morris-dancing was not uncommon in Herefordshire in the earlier part of the present century. It has been practised during the same period in Gloucestershire, Somersetshire, and Wiltshire, and in most of the counties round the metropolis. On the 4th of February, 1886, it was revived at Stratford-on-Avon, and caused much interest.

In the "Journal of the Archæological Association,"[†] it is stated that the morris-dancers who go about from village to village in Derbyshire, about Twelfth Day, have their fool, their Maid Marian (generally a man dressed in woman's clothes, and called "the fool's wife,") and sometimes the hobby-horse. They are dressed up in ribbons and tinsel, but the bells are usually discarded.

In October, 1885, there were six or eight morris-dancers at Northenden, in Cheshire. They had light-coloured trousers, tied with ribbons at the knees, white shirt sleeves, straw hats trimmed with ribbons, and artificial flowers. The music was made by a triangle, fifes, and drums. On the 21st September, 1889, being Stockport wakes, a band of morris-dancers perambulated the streets in the evening, dressed in white stockings, knee-breeches, white shirts trimmed with ribbons, and small caps. They were preceded by a good band of music playing dance tunes, in front of which was a lusty man plying a big whip. In rear was "owd sooty face,"

---

[*] "Dictionary of Archaic and Provincial Words," 1850.
[†] 1852, vol. 7, p. 201.

STOCKPORT MORRIS-DANCER.

with a well-patronised collecting-box. On the following Monday, they paraded Edgeley, preceded by a lurry decorated with arches, and carrying a number of little girls prettily dressed. At the wakes held in 1890, a troop of morris-dancers were habited in black jockey-caps, white shirts, black knee-breeches, blue sashes, white stockings, and shoes. Instead of handkerchiefs they had thick white cords tied to the wrist and knotted at the end.

In the early part of the present century, some hundreds of young men could be seen every autumn in Lancashire dancing the morris. Rush-carts were then numerous, and nearly all had dancers accompanying them. As the number of rush-carts gradually declined, the morris-dancers became less numerous, but some were to be seen at one place or another every year, and are still to be met with. There is a very good troop at Shaw, near Oldham, and another at Mossley. They go about to the various wakes in the neighbourhood, and, with frequent practice, have attained a high degree of skill.

No particular season or occasion appears to have been chosen for the performance of the morris-dance, although it was most in request at the May and Whitsuntide games. It was introduced at any festival or merrymaking, Christmas not excepted. In the Household Accounts of the Kytsons of Hengrave Hall, Suffolk, 1583, there is an item:

"In rewarde to the *morris-dancers*, at my mr. his return into the country, ijs."

Sheriffs, too, had their morris-dancers.*

In the old play of "Jacke Drum's Entertainment" (1601):

"*The taber and pipe strike up a morrice. A shoute within:*
 A lord, a lord, a lord, who!
 Ed.: Oh, a morrice is come, observe our country sports,
 'Tis Whitson tyde, and we must frolick it."

* "Survey of London," edition 1618, 4to., p. 164.

"*Enter the morrice.*

THE SONG.
Skip it, and trip it, nimbly, nimbly,
Tickle it, tickle it lustily,
Strike up the taber, for the wenches' favour,
Tickle it, tickle it lustily.
Let us be seen on Hygate greene,
   To dance for the honour of Holloway.
Since we are come hither, let's spare for no leather,
   To dance for the honour of Holloway."

Warner's "Albion's England" (1602, p. 121) says:—

"At Paske begun our *Morris*, and ere Pentecost our May."

Stow * describes the citizens of London of all estates, in the month of May, "lightly, in every parish, or sometimes two or three parishes joining together, had their several mayings, and did fetch in Maypoles with divers warlike shows, with good archers, *morris-dancers*, and other devices for pastime, all the day long, and toward the evening they had stage plays, and bonfires in the streets."

A tract, of the time of Charles I., entitled "Mythomistes," printed by Henry Seyle, at the "Tiger's Head," in St. Paul's Churchyard, speaks of "the best-taught countrey Morris-dauncer, with all his bells and napkins," as performing at Christmas.

"How they become the Morris, with whose bells
 They ring all in to Whitson Ales, and sweat
 Through twenty scarfs and napkins, till the Hobby-horse
 Tire, and the Maid Marian, resolv'd to jelly,
 Be kept for spoon meat."
   —*Cotgrave's English Treasury of Wit and Language* (1655).†

Stevenson, in his "Twelve Moneths" (1661), speaking of April, tells us : "The youth of the country make ready for the *Morris-dance*, and the merry milk-maid supplies them with ribbands her true love had given her."

* "Survey of London," edition 1603.
† See Shirley's "Lady of Pleasure," 1637, act 1.

In a Whitsun-ale, last kept at Greatworth, Northamptonshire, in 1785, the fool, in a motley garb, with a gridiron, painted or worked with a needle, on his back, carried a stick with a bladder, and a calf's tail. Majordomo, and his lady as Queen of May, and my lord's morris (six in number) were in this procession. They danced round a garlanded maypole. A banquet was served in a barn, and all those who misconducted themselves were obliged to ride a wooden horse, and if still more unruly were put into the stocks, which was termed being my lord's organist.

Miss Baker* describes the celebration of a Whitsun-ale early in the present century, in a barn at King's Sutton, fitted up for the entertainment, in which the lord, as the principal, carried a mace made of silk, finely plaited with ribbons, and filled with spices and perfumes for such of the company to smell as desired it. Six morris-dancers were among the performers.

The number of dancers appears to have been unlimited, ranging from one, in the individual morris, to twenty or thirty at the Lancashire rush-bearings, the number being then limited only by the number of young men in the neighbourhood willing to learn the dance. Chambers says the number was at one time limited to five, but varied considerably at various periods. In the painted window at Betley, of the time of Edward IV., there are eleven characters: Robin Hood, Maid Marian, Friar Tuck, piper, fool, hobby-horse, and five dancers. In the painting, by Vinckenboom, of Richmond Palace, about the end of the reign of James I., a morris-dance is introduced in the foreground, consisting of seven figures: a fool, hobby-horse, piper, Maid Marian, and three other dancers. Peck says this dance was "usually performed abroad by an equal number of young men, who danced in their shirts, with ribands, and little bells about their legs. But here, in England,

* "Glossary of Northamptonshire Words," 1854, vol. 2, pp. 433-4.

THE FOOL.

they have always an odd person besides, being a boy dressed in a girl's habit, whom they call Maid Marian, an old favorite character in the sport." In Israel's print there are nine characters; and Strutt mentions five dancers and two musicians, but this appears to have been a dance of fools.

> "*Four* reapers danced a morrice to oaten pipes."
> —*Spectator*.

And Temple says:

> "There went about the country a set of morris-dancers, composed of *ten* men, who danced, a maid marian, and a tabor and pipe."

The characters of Maid Marian, Robin Hood, the hobby-horse, and Friar Tuck, were omitted in course of time, not being required in the dance. The fool survived, and as "owd sooty face," "dirty Bet," and "owd mollycoddle" is yet known to the spectators of a Lancashire morris-dance.

Beckwith, in his edition of Blount's "Jocular Tenures," says that at Kidlington, Oxfordshire, on the Monday after Whitsun week, there is "a Morisco-dance of men, and another of *women*."

The dress of the morris-dancers varied according to the means and taste of the performers. The principal dancer appears, however, to have been more highly dressed than the others. In the "Blind Beggar of Bednal Green," by John Day, 1659, it is said of one of the characters: "He wants no cloths, for he hath a cloak laid on with gold lace, and an embroidered jerkin; and thus he is marching hither like the foreman of a morris." In the Kingston-upon-Thames accounts, already quoted, the Moor's coat, in 1536-37, was of buckram, whilst those of the dancers were of fustian. The Spanish morris was also danced at puppet-shows by a person habited like a Moor, with castanets; and Du Jon informs us that the morris-dancers usually blackened their faces with soot, that they might the better pass for Moors. In "Pasquill and Marforuis" (1589), Penry, the Welshman, is "the foregallant of the Morrice with the treble belles, shot through the wit with a woodcock's bill."

Stubbes, in his "Anatomie of Abuses," 1585, thus describes the dress of the morris-dancers: "The Lord of Misrule investeth his men with his liveries of greene, yellow, or some other light wanton colour. And, as though they were not gaudy ynough, I should say, they bedecke themselves with scarffes, ribbons, and laces, hanged all over with golde ringes, precious stones, and other jewels; this done, they tie about either legge twentie or fourtie belles, with rich handkerchiefe in their handes, and sometimes laide a crosse over their shoulders and neckes, borrowed for the most part of their pretie *Mopsies* and *Bessies*, for bussing them in the darke."

We have seen, from the Kingston-upon-Thames Churchwardens' Accounts, that in 1536-37 the dresses of the morris-dancers consisted of four coats of white fustian, spangled, and two green satin coats, with garters on which small bells were fastened. The curious old tract, "Old Meg of Herefordshire, for a Mayd Marian, and Hereford Towne, for a Morris-Daunce," etc. (1609), describes the musicians and the twelve dancers, "having long coats of the old fashion, high sleeves gathered at the elbows, and hanging sleeves behind; the stuff, red buffin, striped with white, girdles with white, stockings white, and red roses to their shoes; the one six, a white jews cap, with a jewel and a long red feather; the other, a scarlet jews cap, with a jewel and a white feather; so the hobby-horse, and so the maid-marian was attired in colours. The whifflers* had long staves, white and red."

Scarves, ribbands, and laces, hung all over with gold rings, and even precious stones, are also mentioned in

* Men who kept back the crowd.

the time of Elizabeth.* Miles, the miller of Ruddington, in Sampson's play of "The Vow-breaker, or the Fayre Maid of Clifton" (1636), says he is come to borrow "a few ribbandes, bracelets, eare-rings, wyertyers, and silke girdles, and hand-kerchers for a Morice, and a show before the Queene."

Knee-breeches appear to have been usually worn by the morris-dancers, partly owing to appearance, and partly to convenience in use; but in Alexander Wilson's painting of the rush-cart the dancers have long trousers, shoes, white shirts trimmed with ribbons, and helmet-shaped hats. The costume worn now, and for many years past (colour being left to individual taste, except in the case of the breeches, which are generally of the same colour and material in each band of dancers), consists of shoes with buckles, white stockings, knee-breeches tied with ribbons, a brightly-coloured scarf or sash round the waist, white shirt trimmed with ribbons and fastened with brooches, and white straw hats decorated with ribbons and rosettes. White handkerchiefs, or "streamers," are tied to the wrist.

The early morris-dancers were adorned with small bells:

"The Morrice rings while Hobby-Horse doth foot it featously."
—*Beaumont and Fletcher's "Knight of the Burning Pestle."*

and

" . . . I have seen him
Caper upright like a wild Morisco,
Shaking his bloody darts as he his bells."
—*Shakspeare's "Henry VI.," Part 2, Act iii., Sc. 1.*

At Kingston-upon-Thames, 23 Henry VII., 1531-32, "bellys for the dawnsars" cost 12d. The Churchwardens' Accounts of St. Helen's, Abingdon, Berkshire, contain mention of the morris-bells from the first year of the reign of Philip and Mary (1554-55) to the thirty-fourth of Elizabeth (1592). In 1560, payment was

* Stubbes' "Anatomie of Abuses," 1585; "Knight of the Burning Pestle," act iv.

made for "two dossin of Morres-bells," and they are also mentioned in the Churchwardens' Accounts of St. Mary-at-hill, London.

There is good reason for believing that the morris-bells were borrowed from the genuine *Moorish dance*, a circumstance that tends to corroborate the opinion with respect to the etymology of the *morris*. Among the beautiful habits of various nations, published by Hans Weigel, at Nuremberg, in 1577, there is the

MOORISH LADY DANCING THE MORRIS.

figure of an African lady, of the kingdom of Fez, in the act of dancing, with bells at her feet.

In the preface to "Mythomistes," a tract of the time of Charles I., there is an allusion to the bells in the morris-dance: "Yet such helpes, as if nature have not beforehand in his byrth, given a Poet, all such forced art will come behind as lame to the businesse and deficient as the best-taught countrey Morris-daunser, with all his *bells and napkins*, will ill deserve to be, in an Inne of Courte at Christmas, tearmed the thing they call a fine reveller."

A note signed "Harris," in Reed's edition of "Shakspeare" (1803), informs us that "Morrice-dancing, *with bells on the legs*, is common at this day in Oxfordshire and the adjacent counties, on May Day, Holy Thursday, and Whitsun-Ales, attended by the Fool, or, as he is generally called, the Squire, and also a Lord and Lady, the latter, most probably, the Maid Marian, . . . nor is the Hobby-horse forgot."

Strutt, in his "Sports and Pastimes of the People of England," 1810, observes that the garments of the morris-dancers were adorned with bells, "which were not placed there merely for the sake of ornament, but were to be sounded as they danced. These bells were of unequal sizes, and differently denominated, as the fore bell, the second bell, the treble, the tenor or great bell, and mention is also made of double bells. Sometimes they used trebles only, but these refinements were of later times.* In the third year of the reign of Queen Elizabeth (1561), two dozen of morris-bells were estimated at one shilling."

At first, these bells were small and numerous, and affixed to all parts of the body, the neck, shoulders, elbows, wrists, waist, knee, and ankle; the wrist, knee, and ankle being, however, the principal places. The number of bells round each leg sometimes amounted from twenty to forty. They were occasionally jingled by the hands.

All the Munich morris-dancers have bells, principally at the knees, and this peculiarity is also shown in the Betley window, where the dancers have them at the knees only. In Israel's print they are attached to the wrists and ankles; Kemp wears a broad garter below the knee, with three rows of bells, and this is also the case with the morris-dancer in Vinckenboom's picture. Their use in the English dance seems to have existed only about a century or a little more, and they are now

* See Rowley's "Witch of Edmonton," 1658, act i., sc. 2.

not used, their use seems to be entirely forgotten. Those used in Lancashire were the collar of horse-bells, and were worn round the neck of the fool, who jingled them as he capered about. Napkins or handkerchiefs took the place of the bells, probably from the streamers attached to the sleeves of the dancers, which were slashed and left open. (See Nos. 10 and 11 in the Betley window, and No. 6 of the Munich figures.) These handkerchiefs were attached to the wrist, and are now so used, the graceful manipulation of the arms and handkerchiefs forming a graceful feature in the dance.

The cut above is curious, inasmuch as it shows that the fondness for the handkerchief among the morris-dancers in the middle of the seventeenth century had superseded the use of bells and other ornaments for the hand. The verses beneath give a lively description of the personal appearance of this important character. The cut is copied from Dr. Dibdin's edition of More's "Utopia," vol. 2, p. 266:

"With a noise and a din,
 Comes the Maurice-Dancer in,
With a fine linen shirt, but a buckram skin,
 Oh! he treads out such a peale,
 From his paire of legs of veale,
The quarters are idols to him.
 Nor do those knaves inviron
 Their toes with so much iron,
'Twill ruin a smith to shoe him.

> "Ay, and then he flings about
>   His sweat and his clout.
> The wiser think it two ells,
>   While the yeomen find it meet
> That he jangle at his feet
> The fore-horse's right-eare jewels." *

The following picture is taken from Randle Holmes' curious "Academie of Armorie," iii., p. 109, and shows the mode of using the handkerchief.

The streamers which proceed from the sleeves and flutter in the wind, though continued in very modern times, were anciently not peculiar to morris-dancers, examples of them occurring in many old prints. The

handkerchiefs, or napkins, as they are sometimes called, were held in the hand, or tied to the wrists or shoulders.†

In the "Knave of Hearts" (1612), we read:

> "My *sleeves* are like some Morris-dansing fellow."

The morris-dance of the present day varies greatly from that of the period of its introduction. It is a *progressive* dance, and bears little resemblance either to the Spanish *fandango*, or the Greek *Pyrrho Saltatio*. Sir John Hawkins ‡ describes it as "a dance of young men, in their shirts, with bells at their feet, and ribbands of various colours tied round their arms and flung

---

* "Recreation for Ingenious Head Pieces," etc., edition 1667, 12mo.
† "Knight of the Burning Pestle," act iv.
‡ "General History of Music," 1776, vol. 2, p. 135.

across their shoulders." Dr. Johnson (1785) says it was "a dance in which bells are gingled, or staves or swords clashed, which was learned by the Moors, and was probably a kind of Pyrrhic or military dance;" this, however, seems to bear a greater resemblance to the *sword-dance*, formerly practised in England, than to the morris-dance. Douce states that the *Moorish dance* is "exceedingly different from the *morris-dance* of the present day, it being performed with the castanets or rattles at the ends of the fingers, and not with bells attached to various parts of the dress ; and that it is identical with the *fandango*." The true explanation probably lies in the supposition that the *Moorish dance* was the parent of the *fandango*, which, as it passed through various countries, was modified by its learners, a process which takes place in most things introduced from a foreign country. Time, too, and disuse for long periods, has led to a considerable change in the postures. The introduction of modern musical instruments and tunes has also contributed to the change.

"Come, bustle, lads, for one dance more,
And then *cross morris* three times o'er."
Riding's "*Village Muse*," 1854.

It is not surprising to find so popular a dance as the morris frequently introduced upon the stage. In Nashe's play of "Summers' last Will and Testament," there is a stage direction : "Ver goes in and fetcheth out the Hobby-Horse and the Morrice-Daunce, who daunce about." Afterwards, there enter three clowns and three maids who dance the morris, and at the same time sing the following song :

"Trip and goe, heave and hoe,
Up and downe, to and fro,
From the towne, to the grove,
Two and two, let us rove,
A Maying, a playing ;
Love hath no gainsaying,
So merrily trip and goe."

THE MUSICIANS, 1870

T

In Randolph's "Amyntas," act v., the stage direction is, "Jocastus with a morrice, himselfe Maid-marrion."

From time immemorial the music which marked the time of the morris-dance was provided by the pipe and tabor, and, when the old piper ceased to exist, was continued by a fifer and a drummer down to our own day, a couple of fifers and a drummer being considered the correct thing. Thus in "Much Ado about Nothing:"

"I have known when there was no music with him but the drum and fife, and now he would much rather hear the tabor and pipe."

"John the piper" occurs in some Newton charters about 1346. Drayton ("Eclogue" iii.) observes:

"Myself above Tom Piper to advance,
Who so bestirs him in the Morris-dance,
For penny wage."

In 1585, John Taylor published his "Drinke and Welcome," in which he mentions "the fagge-end of an old man's old will, who gave a good somme of mony to a Red-fac'd Ale-drinker who plaid upon a Pipe and Tabor, which was this: 'To make your Pipe and Tabor keepe their sound, and dye your crimson tincture more profound, There growes no better medicine on the ground Than *Alcano* (if it may be found) To buy which drug I give a hundred pound.'"

These wandering minstrels were a constant source of trouble to the churchwardens by their piping during the time of divine service, and drawing the rabble together. In 1579, a mandate was issued at Manchester against pipers and minstrels making and frequenting bear-baiting and bull-baiting on the Sabbath days, or upon any other days. At a Visitation held at Garstang, 5th August, 1596, "John Baxter, Pyper," was returned contumacious for "that he hath used to Pype uppon the Saboth daie before Even songe." He was ordered to "doe soe noe more hereafter uppon paine of the Lawe, not withstand'g the Judge hath tollerated the s^d John to Pype and Plaie upon Sundaies in the eveninge soe that hee begin nott to Plaie before sixe of the Clocke in the eveninge." And at another Visitation, held at Stockport, 19th September, 1598, " John Baillie" was deemed contumacious "for pypinge in time of Divine Eveninge praier."

In the Stockport Parish Registers, under date 1st January, 1610, is entered the baptism of "ffraunces, sonne of William Hunte, of Stockport, a pyper;" and on the 19th March, 1611, "an infant of William Huntes, of Stockport, pyper," was buried. The name of another Stockport piper occurs on the 11th December, 1625, when "Susanna, a pore chyld of William Hayes, a pyper," was buried.

There are two little tracts relating to the morris-dance, which, from their antiquity and rarity, require to be noticed. The first is entitled: "Kemp's Nine Daies' Wonder," "performed in a daunce from London to Norwich. Containing the pleasure, paines, and kinde entertainment of William Kemp betweene London and that Citty, in his late *Morrice*. Wherein is somewhat set downe worth note; to reproove the slaunders spred of him; many things merry, nothing hurtfull. Written by himselfe to satisfie his friends. London, printed by E. A., for Nicholas Ling, and are to be solde at his shop at the west doore of Saint Paules Church." 1600, 4to., b. l. *

Kemp performed a sort of dancing journey between the two cities in 1599, which caused such a sensation that he was induced to print an account of it in 1600,

---

* Of the original edition, only one copy, a quarto of about twenty pages, is known, and is in the Bodleian Library, Oxford. In 1840, it was reprinted for the Camden Society, with notes by the Rev. A. Dyce; and, in 1884, Mr. Edmund Goldsmid, F.R.H.S., reprinted it in the "Collectanea Adamantæa" series of reprints, also with notes. An interesting article on "Will Kemp, and his Dance from London to Norwich," with a facsimile of the woodcut, is given in Walford's "Antiquarian," 1886, vol. 10, pp. 241-250.

KEMP DANCING THE MORRIS, 1600.

dedicated to "Mistris Anne Fitton,"[*] one of Queen Elizabeth's maids of honour. The title-page is adorned with a woodcut, representing Kemp dancing, and his attendant, Tom the Piper, playing on the pipe and tabor, whom Kemp, in his book, calls Thomas Slye, his taborer.

Kemp started from London at seven in the morning, on the first Monday in Lent, and, after various adventures, reached Romford that night, where he rested during Tuesday and Wednesday. He started again on Thursday morning, and made an unfortunate beginning by straining his hip, but he continued his progress, attended by a great number of spectators, and on Saturday morning reached Chelmsford, where the crowd assembled to receive him was so great that it took him an hour to make his way through them to his lodgings. At this town, where Kemp remained till Monday, an incident occurred which curiously illustrates the popular taste for the morris-dance at that time :

"At Chelmsford, a mayde not passing fourteene years of age, dwelling with one Sudley, my kinde friend, made request to her master and dame that she might daunce the Morrice with me in a great large roome. They being intreated, I was soone wonne to fit her with bels ; besides, she would have the olde fashion, with napking on her armes ; and to our jumps we fell. A whole houre she held out ; but then being ready to lye downe, I left her off ; but thus much in her praise, I would have challenged the strongest man in Chelmsford, and amongst many I thinke few would have done so much."

Other challenges of this kind, equally unsuccessful, took place on Monday's progress, and on the Wednesday of the second week, which was Kemp's fifth day of labour, in which he danced from Braintree, through

[*] Mr. Goldsmid, in his reprint, assumes this to have been a mistake, and that her name was Mary ; but the fact is, there were two sisters, Ann and Mary Fitton, both of whom were maids of honour to Queen Elizabeth. They were the daughters of Sir Edward Fitton, Knt., of Gawsworth, co. Chester, by Alice, daughter and heiress of Sir John Holcroft, Knt., of Holcroft, co. Lancaster. Anne married, about 1595, Sir John Newdegate, Knt., of Erbury, co. Warwick. Mary married, first, William Polwhele, gent., and secondly, Captain Lougher.

Sudbury, to Melford. He relates the following incidents :

"In this towne of Sudbury there came a lusty, tall fellow, a butcher by his profession, that would, in a Morrice, keepe me company to Bury. I, being glad of his friendly offer, gave him thankes, and forward wee did set ; but, ere ever wee had measur'd half-a-mile of our way, he gave me over in the plain field, protesting that, if he might get a 100 pound, he would not hold out with me ; for, indeed, my pace in dancing is not ordinary. As he and I were parting, a lusty country lasse being among the people, call'd him faint-hearted lout, saying, 'If I had begun to daunce, I would have held out one myle, though it had cost my life.' At which words many laughed. 'Nay,' saith she, 'if the daunger will lend me a leash of his bells, I'le venter to treade one myle with him myselfe.' I lookt upon her, saw mirth in her eies, heard boldness in her words, and beheld her ready to tucke up her russat petticoate, I fitted her with bels, which she merrily taking, garnisht her thick, short legs, and, with a smooth brow, bade the tabrer begin. The drum strucke, forward marcht I with my merry Mayde Marian, who shooke her fat sides, and footed it merrily to Melford, being a long myle. There parting with her (besides her skinfull of drinke), and English crowne to buy more drinke, for, good wench, she was in a pittious heate. My kindness she requited with dropping some dozen of short curtsies, and bidding God blesse the dancer. I bade her adieu, and, to give her her due, she had a good eare, daunst truly, and wee parted friends."

Having been the guest of "Master Colts," of Melford, from Wednesday night to Saturday morning, Kemp made on this day another day's progress. Many gentlemen of the place accompanied him the first mile. "Which myle," says he, "Master Colts his foole would needs daunce with me, and had his desire, where leaving me, two fooles parted faire in a foule way. I, keeping on my course to Clare, where I a while rested, and then cheerfully set forward to Bury." He reached Bury that evening, and was shut up there by an unexpected accident, so heavy a fall of snow that he was unable to continue his progress until the Friday following. This Friday of the third week since he left London, was only his seventh days' dancing, and he had so well reposed, that he performed the ten miles, from Bury to Thetford, in three hours, arriving at the latter town a little after ten in the forenoon. "But, indeed, considering how I had been booted the other journeys before, and that all this way, or the most of it, was over a heath, it was no great wonder, for I far'd like one that had escaped the stockes, and tride the use of his legs to out-run the constable, so light was my heeles, that I counted the ten myle as a leape." At Thetford, he was hospitably entertained by Sir Edwin Rich, from Friday evening to Monday morning, and this worthy knight, "to conclude liberally as hee had began and continued, at my departure on Monday, his worship gave me five pounds," a considerable sum at that time. On Monday, Kemp danced to Hingham through very bad roads, and frequently interrupted by the hospitality or importunity of the people of the road. On Wednesday of the fourth week, Kemp reached Norwich, but the crowd which came out of the city to receive him, was so great, that, tired as he was, he resolved not to dance into it that day, and he rode on horseback into the city, where he was received in a very flattering manner by the mayor, Master Roger Weld. It was not till Saturday that Kemp's dance into Norwich took place, his journey from London having thus taken exactly four weeks, of which period nine days were occupied in dancing the morris.[*]

The second tract was printed in 1609 (4to.), and bears the curious title of "*Old Meg of Herefordshire, for a Mayd Marian, and Hereford Towne for a Morris Daunce; or Twelve Morris Dauncers in Herefordshire of Twelve Hundred Years Old.*" It is dedicated: "*To that renowned Ox-leach, Old Hall, Taborer of Herefordshire, and to his most invincible, weather-beaten, Nutbrowne Tabor, being alreadie old and sound, threescore yeares and upward. To thee (old Hall), that for thy Age and Art mightest have cured an Oxe that was

[*] Chambers's "Book of Days," 1863, vol. 1, pp. 632-3.

eaten at Saint Quintins, that for thy warlike musicke
mightest have strucke up at Bullen, when great
Drummes wore broken heads, thy little continuall
Taber had been enough to have put spirit into all the
souldiers: Now, Twevie-pipe, that famous Southern
Taberer with the Cowleyan windpipe, who for whuling
hath beene famous through the Globe of the world, did
never gain such renowne and credite by his pipe and
Taber, as thou (old *Hall*), by striking up to these
twelve hundred yeares Morris-daunters: Nor art thou
alone (sweet *Hall*) a most exquisite Taber-man, but an
excellent Oxe-leach, and canst pleasure thy neighbours.
The people of Herefordshire are beholding to thee, thou
guist the men light hearts by thy Pype, and the women
light heeles by thy Taber: O wonderful Pyper, O
admirable Taber-man, make use of thy worth, even
after death, that art so famously worthy in thy life,
both for thy age, skill, and thy onbruized Taber, who
these threescore yeares has kept—sound and oneract,—
neither lost her first voyce, or her fashion: once for the
countrye's pleasure imitate that Bohemian *Trisui*,
who at his death gave his Souldiers a strict command,
to flea his skin off, and cover a drum with it, that alive
and dead, he might sound like a terror in the ears of
his enemies: so thou, sweet *Hereford Hall*, bequeath
in thy last will thy velom-spotted skin, to cover Tabors:
at the sound of which to set all the shires a dauncing."

The account then opens: "The courts of kings for
stately measures: the city for light heels, and nimble
footing: the country for shuffling dances: western
men for gambols: Middlesex men for tricks above
ground: Essex men for the hay: Lancashire for horn-
pipes: Worcestershire for bagpipes: but Herefordshire, for the morris-dance, puts down, not only all
Kent, but very near (if one had line enough to measure
it) three-quarters of Christendom. Never had Saint
Sepulchres a truer ring of bells: never did any silk-

weaver keep braver time with the knocke of the heel: never had the dauncing-horse a better tread of the toe: never could Beverley fair give money to a more sound taborer, nor ever had Robin Hood a more deft Mayd-Marian."

Thus much for the honour of Herefordshire. The preceding paragraphs afford a specimen of the orthography, and the succeeding extracts, duly abbreviated, or with the spelling modernised, will give a fair notion of this remarkable performance:

"Understand, therefore, that in the merriest month of the year which last did take his leave of us, and in that month, as some report, lords went a-Maying, the spring brought forth, just about that time, a number of knights, squires, and gallants, of the best sort, from many parts of the land, to meet at a horse-race near Hereford, in Herefordshire. The horses having, for that year, run themselves well nigh out of breath, wagers of great sums, according to the fashion of such pastimes, being won and lost, and the sports growing to the end, and shutting up, some wit, riper than the rest, fed the stomachs of all men, then and there present, with desire and expectation of a more fresh and lively meeting in the same place, to be performed this year of 1609. The ceremonies which their meeting was to stand upon were these, that every man should engage himself, under his hand, to bring, this present year, to the place appointed, running horses for the race, cocks of the game to maintain battles, etc., with good store of money, to fly up and down between those that were to lay wagers. He that first gave fire to this sociable motion, undertook to bring a 'hobby-horse' to the race that should outrun all the nags which were to come thither, and hold out in a longer race."

When the time arrived, "Expectation did, within few days, make Hereford town show like the best peopled city. Inns were lodgings for lords. Baucis and Philemon's house (had it stood there) would have been taken up for a knight. The streets swarmed with people, staring, and joyfully welcoming whole bravies of gallants, who came bravely flocking on horseback, like so many lusty adventurers. Bath made her waters to boil up, and swell like a spring-tide, with the overflowing of her own tears, to see her dearest guests leave her for the love of a horse-race at Hereford, the number of them being, at least, two or three hundred. Amongst many of the better ranks, these marched with the foremost: lord Herbert, of Ragland, sir Thomas Somerset, Charles Somerset, count Arundel's two sons, sir Edward Swift, sir Thomas Mildemay, sir Robert Taxley, sir Robert Carey, sir John Philpot, sir Ed. Lewes, sir Francis Lacon, sir James Scudamore, sir Thomas Cornwall, sir Robert Boderham, sir Thomas Russell, sir — Bascarvile, sir Thomas Conisby, sir George Chute. These were but a small handful to those rich heaps that were gathered together. But by these, that had the honor to be the leaders, you may guess what numbers were the followers."

At the appointed day, "there was as much talking, and as much preparation for the 'hobby-horse' promised the last year, as about dietting the fairest gelding this year, upon whose head the heaviest wagers were laid. To perform a race of greater length, of greater labor, and yet in shorter time, and by feeble, unexercised, and unapt creatures, that would be an honor to him that undertook it, that would be to Herefordshire a glory, albeit, it might seem an impossibility. Age is nobody in trials of the body, when youth is in place. It gives the other the bucklers, it stands and gives aim, and is content to see youth act, while age sits but as a spectator; because the one does but study and play over the parts which the other hath discharged in this great and troublesome theatre. It was, therefore, now plotted to lay the scene in age, to have the old comedy presented, fathers to be the actors, and beardless boys the spectators. Sophocles, because he was accused of imbecility and dotage, should rehearse his Œdipus Coloneus, while the senate, and his own wild-brain sons, stood by, and were the audience; and to set out this scene with mirth, as well as with wonder, the state of the whole act was put into a morris-dance."

Now, then, to set forth these performers and their show, as nearly as may be, in the language of the old narrator:

THE MORRIS AND ITS OFFICERS.

Two *musicians* were appointed to strike up, and to give the alarm. The one of them (*Squire* of Hereford), was a squire born, and all his sons squires in their cradles. His instrument, a treble violin, upon which he played any old lesson that could be called for, the division he made on the strings being more pleasing than the diapason. "In skill he outshines blind Moore, of London, and hath outplayed more fiddlers than now sneak up and down into all the taverns there. They may all call him their father, or, if you reckon the years rightly which are scored upon his head, the musicians' grandsire, for this tuneable *squire* is 108 years old. Next to him went old *Harrie Rudge*, the taborer. This was old *Hall*, of Hereford. The waits of three metropolitan cities make not more music than he can, with his pipe and tabor, if, at least, his head be hard-braced with nappie ale. This noble old *Hall*, seeing that Apollo was both a fidler and a quack-salver, being able to cure diseases, as well as to harp upon one string, would needs be free of two companies as well (that is to say), the sweet company of musicians, and that other, which deals in salves and plasters, for he both beats a tabor, with good judgment, and (with better) can help an ox if he find himself ill at ease.

The wood of this old *Hall's* tabor should have been made a pail to carry water in, at the beginning of king Edward the sixth's reign; but *Hall*, being wise, because he was, even then, reasonably well stricken in years, saved it from going to the water, and converted it, in those days, to a tabor. So that his tabor hath made bachelors and lasses dance round about the May-pole threescore summers, one after another, in order, and is yet not worm-eaten. And noble *Hall* himself hath stood (like an oak), in all storms, by the space of fourscore and seventeen winters, and is not yet falling to the ground."

WHIFFLERS.—The marshals of the field were four. These had no great stomach to dance in the morris, but took upon them the office of whifflers. 1. *Thomas Price*, of Clodacke, a subsidy man,* and one upon whose cheeks age had written 105 years. 2. *Thomas Andros*, of Begger Weston, a subsidy man, for he carried upon his back the weighty burden of 108 years. 3. *William Edwards*, of Bodenham (his name is in the king's books likewise), and unto him had time also given the use of 108 years; and, besides the blessings of so many years, the comfort of a young wife, and, by that wife, a child of six years old. 4. *John Sanders*, of Wolford, an ironworker, the hardness of which labour carried him safely over the high hill of old age, where she bestowed upon him 102 years. These four *whifflers*, casting up what all their days, which they had spent in the world, could make, found that they amounted to 423 years, so that if the rest of their dancing brotherhood had come short of their account, and could not (every man) make up one hundred years, these offered were able to lend them three-and-twenty years; but the others had enough of their own, and needed not to borrow of any man.

See how the *morris-dancers* bestir their legs. Lift

---

* One assessed on the *Subsidy Roll*, a wealthy person.

up your eyes, leap up behind their heads that stand before you, or else get upon stalls, for I hear their bells, and behold, here they come :

1. Of *twelve* in the whole team, the foreman was *James Tomkins*, of Lengerren, a gentleman by birth, neither loved of fortune, nor hated of her, for he was never so poor as to be pitied, nor ever so rich as to be envied. When fourscore and eighteen years old he married a wife of two-and-fifty years old ; " she brought him a child that is now eight years old (living), the father himself having now the glass of his life running to fill up the full number of 106 yeares."

2. After him comes, lustily dancing, *John Willis*, of Dormington, a bone-setter, his dancing fit to his weight of ninety-seven years. " His purpose in being one of the Morris was both honest and charitable, for he bestowed his person upon them, with intent to be ready at hand if any dislocation should be wrought upon any joynt in his old companions by fetching lofty tricks which, by all means possible, they were sworn to avoid."

3. Room for little *Dick Phillips*, of Middleton. How nimbly he shakes his heels! Well danced, old heart of oak ; and yet, as little as he seems, his courage is as big as the hobby-horse's, for the fruits of his youth, gathered long agon, are not yet withered. His eldest son is at this present fourscore years of age, and his second son may now reckon threescore ; at our lady-day last, he made up the years of his life just 102.

4. Now falls into his right place *William Waiton*, of Marden, with 102 years at his heels. " He was an old fisher, and of a clean man an excellent fowler."

5. Here slips in *William Mosse*, who, contrary to his name, had no moss at his heels. He bears the age of 106.

6. Now cast your eyes upon *Thomas Winney*, of Holmer, an honest subsidy man, dwelling close by the

town. "He dances with 100 years about him, wheresoever he goes, if the churchyard and cramp take him not."

7. But how like you *John Lace*, of Madley, a tailor, and an excellent name for it? "In his youth he was a hosier—born before the dissension between cloth breeches and velvet breeches, he carries fourscore and seventeen summers about him, and faine would borrow three years of James Tomkins [the foreman] to make him an hundred; and James may very well spare them, and yet leave three toward the interest."

8. But what say you to *John Careless*? "You let him passe by you, and seem as careless as he, a man of fourscore and sixteen at Midsummer next. He hath been a dweller in Homlacie threescore years and two, and known to be a tall man, till now he begins to be crooked, but for a body and a beard he becomes any Morris in Christendom."

9. At the heels of him follows his fellow, *William Maio*, of Egelton, an old soldier, and now a lusty labourer, and a tall man. "Forty years since, being grievously wounded, he carried his liver and his lights home half a mile, and you may still put your finger into them, but for a thin skin over them; and for all these storms he arrives at fourscore and seventeen, and dances merrily."

10. But look you who comes: "*John Hunt*, the *Hobby-horse*, wanting but three of an hundred, 'twere time for him to forget himself, and sing but *O, nothing but O, the hobby-horse is forgotten*. The Maid-marian, following him, offers to lend him seven years more, but if he would take up ten in the hundred his company are able to lend them."

11. But now give way for the *Maid Marian*, old "*Meg Goodwin*, the famous wench of Erdistand, of whom Master Weaver, of Burton, that was fourscore and ten years old, was wont to say she was twenty years older

than he, and he died ten years since. This old *Meg* was at Prince Arthur's death, at Ludlow, and had her part in the *dole*. She was threescore years (she saith) a maid, and twenty years otherwise, that's what you will, and since hath been thought fit to be a Maid-marian, at the age of 120."

12. Welcome *John Mando*. He was born at Cradly. A very good two-hand sword man, of the age of one hundred, on black Monday last, and serves in place of Morgan Deede, who climbs to that age within four years, here present dwelling in the town; but he has a great desire to keep his bed and be spared.

These eighteen persons, the fiddler, the taborer, the four whifflers, and the twelve dancers in this morris carried about them 1837 years. "And, for a good wager, it were easy to find, in Herefordshire, four hundred persons more within three years over or under an hundred years; yet the shire is no way four-and-twenty miles over."

For the fashion observed amongst the musicians, and the habit of the dancers, take a view of both. "The musicians and the twelve dancers had long coats of the old fashion, high sleeves gathered at the elbows, and hanging sleeves behind; the stuff, red buffin, striped with white, girdles with white, stockings white, and red roses to their shoes; the one six, a white jews cap with a jewel and a long red feather; the other, a scarlet jews cap with a jewel and a white feather; so the hobby-horse, and so the maid-marian was attired in colours; the whifflers had long staves, white and red. After the dance was ended, diverse courtiers, that won wagers at the race, took those colours and wore them in their hats."

The Speech before the Morris.

"Ye servants of our mighty king,
That came from court one hundred mile
To see our race, and sport this spring,
Ye are welcome, that is our country stile,

"And much good do you, we are sorry
That *Hereford* hath no better for you.
   A horse, a cock, trainsents, a bull,
   Primero, gleek, hazard, mumchance ;
These sports through time are grown so dull,
As good to see a Morris-dance,
Which sport was promised in jest,
But paid as truly as the rest.
A race (quoth you) behold a race,
No race of horses, but of men.
Men born not ten miles from this place,
Whose courses outrun hundreds ten.
A thousand years on ten men's backs,
And one supplies what other lacks.

      L'envoy.

This is the *L'envoy* (you may gather)
Gentlemen, yeomen, grooms, and pages,
Let's pray, Prince *Henry* and his father
May outlive all these ten men's ages.
And he that mocks this application
Is but a knave past reformation."

After this speech, "old *Hall* struck up, and the Morris-dancers fell to footing, whilst the whifflers in their office made room for the hobby-horse."

The narrative concludes by inquiring: "And how do you like this Morris-dance of Herefordshire? Are they not brave old youths? Have they not the right footing, the true tread, comely lifting up one leg, and active bestowing of the other? Kemp's morris to Norwich was no more to this then a gaillaird, on a common stage, at the end of an old dead comedy, is to a coranto danced on the ropes. Here is a dozen of younkers, that have hearts of oak at fourscore years, backs of steel at fourscore and ten, ribs of iron at a hundred, bodies sound as bells, and healthful (according to the Russian proverb) as an ox, when they are travelling down the hill to make that 120. These shewed in their dancing, and moving up and down, as if Mawlborne hills, in the very depth of winter—all their heads covered with snow—shook and danced at some earthquake. Shall any man lay blame on these good old fathers, because at such years they had not spent all their wild oats? No, we commend (as Tully saith) a young man that smells somewhat of the old signior, and can but counterfeit gravity in his cheeks; and shall we not heave up with praises an old man that at 108 years' end can rake his dead embers abroad, and show some coals of the lusty *Juventus* glowing in him even then? Such an old madcap deserves better to be the stuffing of a chronicle, than Charing Cross does for loosing his rotten head, which (through age, being wind shaken) fell off, and was trod upon in contempt. Were old Stowe alive, here were taboring work enough for his pen; but, howsoever, so memorable a monument of man shall not wither in oblivion, if the sweet April showers, which drop from the Muse's water, can make it grow up and flourish. A dishonour were it to poets and all pen-men if acts of this worth should not encomiastically be celebrated and recorded. Oh! if all the people in the kingdom should have their days stretched out to the length of these men, clerks and sextons might go and hang themselves in the bell ropes, they would have cold doings; prodigal heirs might beg, they should hardly find an almanack that would tell them when their lands should come to their hands by the death of their fathers, for they themselves would have white beards before they could arrive at their full age. It were no hoping after dead men's shoes, for both upper leather and soles would be worn out to nothing. As great pity it were *(Old Margaret,* or rather new *Mayd-Marian)* that all men's wives (especially those that like dutch-watches have alarums in their mouths) should last so long as thou hast done, how would the world be plagued? Alas! what do I see? Hold, *Taborer!* stand, *Hobby-horse! Morris-dancers*, lend us your hands! Behold one of the nimble-legged old gallants is by chance fallen down,

and is either so heavy, so weary, so inactive of himself,
or else five of his fellows are of such little strength,
that all their arms are put under him, as levers, to lift
him up, yet the good old boys cannot set him on his
feet. Let him not lie for shame, you that have, all this
while, seen him dance, and though he be a little out of
his part, in the very last act of all, yet hiss at nothing,
but rather, *Summi Jovis causa plaudite.*" *

This dance is referred to in Sir William Temple's
"Miscellanea," part 3, Essay on Health and Long
Life; and Howell, in his "Parly of Beasts," 1660, p.
122, also alludes to it.

Brand states that a few years ago a May-game, or
morris-dance, was performed by the following eight
men, in Herefordshire, whose ages, computed together,
amounted to 800 years: J. Corley, aged 109; Thomas
Buckley, 106; John Snow, 101; John Edey, 104;
George Bailey, 106; Joseph Medbury, 100; John
Medbury, 95; Joseph Pidgeon, 79.

* Hone's "Year Book," 1832, pp. 418-422.

The Wakes.

"So blithe and bonny now the lads and lasses are,
That ever, as anon the bagpipe up doth blow,
Cast in a gallant round about the hearth they go,
And, at each pause, they kiss—was never seen such rule
In any place but here, at bonfire, or at Yule;
And every village smokes at wakes with lusty cheer,
Then, 'Hey' (they cry), 'for Lun and Lancasheere,'
That one high hill was heard to tell it to his brother,
That instantly agreed to tell it to some other."
—DRAYTON.

IGILS, or wakes, are of great antiquity, probably cœval with Christianity itself. Nelson, in his "Companion for the Festivals and Fasts of the Church of England,"* has many references to them, from which we gather that vigils, from the Latin word *vigilæ*, signify watchings, it being the custom, in primitive times, to pass a great part of the night that preceded certain holy days in devotion and religious exercises, and this even in those places which they set apart for the public worship of God. But when these night meetings came to be so far abused that no care could prevent several disorders and irregularities, the Church thought fit to abolish them, and these night-watches were converted into fasts, still keeping the former name of vigils. The early Christians, who generally apprehended that the end of the world was near at hand, employed part of the night in watching and prayer, expecting that at midnight the cry would be made, "Behold, the Bride-

* 1757, pp. 563-566.

groom cometh!" Others have referred the rise of these night-watches to the necessity Christians were under of meeting in the night for the exercise of their religion, in order to avoid persecution by their enemies. Tertullian confirms the custom of frequenting the assemblies for religious worship, and of receiving the Eucharist before day, and Pliny, in the account he gave to the emperor concerning the Christians, their meeting before day to sing hymns to our Saviour, etc., makes a part of it. When persecution ceased, and Christians had the liberty of performing their devotions in a more public manner, they still continued their night-watches before great festivals, particularly that of Easter. This practice was in great vigour in the time of St. Jerome, who defended these vigils against the objections of Vigilantius, who endeavoured to have them abolished, on the ground of the disorders committed at them. The council of Eliberis, held *anno* 305, forbade the admission of women, to prevent the ill consequences of these promiscuous assemblies, but they were not abolished till after St. Jerome's time, nor, as some think, till the beginning of the sixth century.

Strutt, in his "Sports and Pastimes of the People of England," 1810, says the wakes greatly resembled the *agapæ*, or love-feasts, of the early Christians, and quotes an old writer, who says:

"And ye shal understond and know how the Evyns were first found in old time. In the begynning of holy Churche, it was so that the people cam to the Churche with candellys burnyng, and would wake, and come toward night to the church in their devocion; and, afterwards, the pepull fell to letcherie, and songs and daunses, with harping and piping, and also to glotony and sinne; and so tourned the holyness of cursydness; wherefore holy faders ordeyned the pepull to leve that waking and to fast the evyn, but it is called vigilia, that is, waking, in English, and eveyn, for of eveyn they were wont to come to churche."

On the conversion of the Saxons by St. Augustine, the heathen Paganalia were, with some modifications, continued among the converts, by an order of Pope Gregory the Great, written about the year 601, to Mellitus, the Abbot who accompanied St. Augustine in his mission hither. His words are to this effect: "On the day of dedication, or the suffering days of holy martyrs, whose relics are there deposited, they may build themselves booths of the boughs of the trees about those churches which have been turned to that use from temples, and celebrate the solemnity with religious feasting, and no more offer beasts to the devil."

The 28th Canon, established by King Edgar, ordered those who came to the wake to pray devoutly, and not to betake themselves to drunkenness and debauchery. The festival of the day on which the church of any parish was dedicated, is also specially enjoined in the law of Edward the Confessor.

"Wake," says the "Imperial Dictionary," "is the feast of the dedication of the parish church, formerly kept by watching all night.* At present, most fast days are popularly called *wakes* in the rural districts of England, but the peculiar wake of country parishes was originally the day of the week on which the church had been dedicated, afterwards the day of the year. Every rural parish had its wake every year, and most of them had two wakes, one on the day of dedication, and another on the birthday of the saint to whom the church was dedicated. The festival of the dedication has long since been entirely discontinued, whilst the saints' day festival still subsists in some of the rural districts of England, in the altered form of a *country wake*."

In proportion as these festivals deviated from the original design of their institution, they became more popular, the conviviality was extended, and not only the inhabitants of the parish to which the church be-

---

* Dr. Johnson, in his "Dictionary," 1785, gives a similar origin.

longed were present at them, but they were joined by
others from the neighbouring towns and parishes, who
flocked together on these occasions, and the greater
the reputation of the tutelar saint, the greater, generally,
was the promiscuous assembly. The pedlars and
hawkers attended to sell their wares, and so, by
degrees, the religious wake was converted into a
secular fair. Booths were erected, often in the churchyard, though this use of the churchyards had been

A COUNTRY WAKE (BULKINGTON, WARWICKSHIRE).

frequently forbidden by Church councils, beginning
from the time of Edward I.*

The riot and debaucheries which eventually took
place at these nocturnal meetings, became so offensive
to religious persons that they were suppressed, and
regular fairs established to be held on the saints' day,
or upon some other day near to it, as might be most
convenient (*Strutt*). The Abbot of Ely, in King

* Bourne "Antiq. Vulg.," 1777.

John's reign, inveighed heavily against the practice of holding these fairs on the Sunday, but it was not entirely abolished until the reign of Henry VI.

At first the feast was regularly kept on the day in every week on which the church was dedicated. Many of the churches being dedicated to the Holy Trinity, Trinity Sunday was the principal day throughout the country for holding these festivals, but upon complaint that the number of holidays was excessively increased, to the detriment of civil government and secular affairs, and upon the discovery that the great irregularities which had crept into these festivities by degrees, especially in churches, chapels, and churchyards, were highly injurious to piety, virtue, and good manners, both statutes and canons were made to regulate and restrain them, and, by an Act of Convocation passed by Henry VIII. in the year 1536, their number was considerably reduced. The feast of the dedication of every church was ordered to be kept upon one and the same day everywhere; that is, on the first Sunday in October, to the total abolition of the observance of the particular saint's day *(Brand)*. The Act caused much dissatisfaction, and in many parts of the country was totally disregarded.

In Manchester, during these holidays, the pageants of Robin Hood, Maid Marian, and Friar Tuck, were exhibited in the church, and were generally got up by the priests. The expense of these exhibitions were defrayed by the churchwardens, who made collections from house to house for that object. After the passing of this Act, the wakes were removed from the church to the churchyard.

In 1579, an assembly of ecclesiastical commissioners, consisting of Henry, Earl of Derby, Henry, Earl of Huntington, and William, Bishop of Chester, held at Manchester, issued a mandate against pipers and minstrels making and frequenting bear-baiting and bull-baiting on the Sabbath days, or upon any other days, and also against superstitious ringing of bells, *wakes*, and common feasts, drunkenness, gaming, and other vicious and unprofitable pursuits.

Stubbes, in his "Anatomie of Abuses," 1585, speaking of wakes and feasts, says: "This is their order therein: Every towne, parish, and village, some at one time of the yeare, some at an other (but, so that every one keeps his proper day, assigned and appropriate to itselfe, which they call their wake day), useth to make great preparation and provision for goode cheare, to which all their friendes and kinsfolkes, farre and neere, are invited." He adds that there are such doings at them "insomuch as the poore men that beare the charges of these Feastes and Wakeses are the poorer, and keep the worser houses a long tyme after. And no marvaile, for many spend more at one of these Wakeses than in all the whole yere besides."

In Ben Jonson's play of "Bartholomew Fair," 1614, a zealous puritan, rejoicing in the name of Zeal-of-the-Land-Busy, when in the stocks at the fair, describes himself as "One that rejoiceth in his affliction, and sitteth here to prophesy the destruction of Fairs and May-games, Wakes, and Whitson-ales, and doth sigh and groan for the reformation of these abuses."

In 1632, the Lord Chief Justice Richardson and Baron Denham were on circuit in Somersetshire, where wakes and ales abounded, and took action, with the general consent of the whole Bench, ordering that these festivals should be altogether suppressed.* This order led to great commotion,† and, to settle the difficulty, Laud, by direction of Charles I., wrote a letter, dated 4th October, 1633, to Pierce, the Bishop of Bath and Wells, to enquire into the management of

---

* Kennet, "Parochial Antiquities," 1818, ii., p. 309.
† To counteract the order issued by the judges to the clergy, the king ordered his declaration of the 18th October, 1633, to be read in the churches on the 2nd February in every year. See Govett's, "The King's Book of Sports," 1890, p. 106.

the wakes and other festivals.* Pierce summoned seventy-two of the better sort of clergy, who, in November of the same year, certified "that on the festivals (which commonly fell on the Sunday) Divine Service was most solemnly performed, and the congregation fuller, both in the forenoon and in the afternoon, than upon any other Sunday; that the clergy desired they might be continued, and that the people, in most places, were of the same sentiment. They believed these annual solemnities serviceable for preserving the memory of the dedication of the churches, for taking up differences by the meeting of friends, for cultivating a good correspondence among neighbours, and for refreshing the poor with the entertainments made upon those anniversaries."†

On the 18th October, 1633, Charles I. issued his warrant, in which "His Majesty finds that, under pretence of taking away abuses, there hath been a general forbidding, not only of ordinary meetings, but of the Feasts of the Dedications of the Churches, commonly called Wakes. Now, his Majesty's express will and pleasure is that these Feasts, with others, shall be observed, and that his Justices of the Peace, in their several Divisions, shall look to it, both that all disorders there may be prevented or punished, and that all neighbourhood and freedom, with manlike and lawful exercises, be used."

A note by Laud, giving the causes of the publication of this declaration or warrant, says: "A great distemper in Somersetshire, upon the forbidding of the Wakes, in sourness of this opinion: An Act of the Judge, that rid that circuit, March 15, 1627, and followed by another, 1630, and his Majesty troubled with petitions and motions of some of the chief men in that county, on both sides."‡

* "Calendar of State Papers," 1633, p. 231.
† Rushworth's "Historical Collections."
‡ Prynne's "Canterburie's Doom," 1646, p. 148.

In Hinde's "Life of John Bruen, of Bruen-Stapleford, in the County of Chester, Esquire," 1641, the author, speaking of Popish and profane wakes at Tarvin, says: "Popery and Profannes, two sisters in evil, had consented and conspired in this parish, as in many other places, together to advance their Idols against the Arke of God, and to celebrate their solemne Feastes of their Popish Saints, as being the *Dii Tutelares*, the *speciall Patrons and Protectors of their Church and Parish*, by their *Wakes* and *Vigils*, kept in commemoration and honour of them, in all riot and excesse of eating and drinking, dalliance and dancing, sporting and gaming, and other abominable impieties and idolatries."

Sir Aston Cokain's "Small Poems of Divers Sorts," 1658, has the following:

"The Zealots here are grown so ignorant,
That they mistake Wakes for some ancient Saint,
They else would keep that Feast ; for though they all
Would be cal'd Saints here, none in heaven they call."

Smith, who wrote an account of the manners and customs of the inhabitants of Cheshire, about the year 1600,[*] says: "Touching their House-keeping, it is bountiful and comparable with any other shire in the realm, and that is to be seen at their Weddings and Burials, *but chiefly at their Wakes*, which they yearly hold, although it be of late years well laid down."

In "A Serious Dissuasive against Whitsun Ales," 1736, a postcript adds: "What I have now been desiring you to consider as touching the evil and pernicious consequence of Whitsun Ales among us, doth also obtain against . . . the ordinary violations of those festival seasons commonly called *Wakes*. And these latter, in particular, have been oftentimes the

[*] Printed in King's "Vale Royall of England, or the County Palatine of Chester Illustrated," 1656.

occasion of the profanation of the Lord's Day, by the bodily exercise of wrestling and cudgel-playing, where they have been suffered to be practised on that holiday."

The Bishop of Chester, Dr. Jayne, preaching at Astbury Church on the 5th of October, 1890, regarded "the venerable institution, known as Astbury Wakes, as a reunion by which old associations, old friendships, were revived, old memories awakened and renewed, and an institution by which that sad tendency, that centrifugal tendency of the present day, to break away from the centre and forget old ties and claims, would be counteracted."

Dr. Gower, in his "Sketch of the Materials for a History of Cheshire," 1771, tells us: "I cannot avoid reminding you, upon the present occasion, that Frumenty makes the principal entertainment of all our Country *Wakes*—our common people call it 'Firmitry.' It is an agreeable composition of boiled wheat, milk, spice, and sugar."

The hospitality exercised at the wakes is noticed by Tusser:

"Fill oven full of flawnes, Ginnie passe not for sleepe,
To-morrow thy father his *wake-daie* will keepe."

It is used in the same sense in "Hamlet," i., 4:

"The king doth *wake* to-night, and take his rouse."

And in King's "Art of Cookery":

"Sometimes the vulgar will of mirth partake,
And have excessive doings at their *wake*."

Mention has been made of the frequency with which old customs are referred to by the old dramatists and poets. The wake consequently comes under notice:

"By dimpled brook and fountain brim,
The wood-nymphs deckt with daisies trim
Their merry *wakes* and pastimes keeps."
                                    Milton.

And Dryden:

> ". . . Putting all the Grecian actors down,
> And winning at the *wake* their parsley crown."

The "Government of the Tongue" speaks of "the droiling peasant who scarce thinks there is any world beyond his village, nor gaiety beyond that of a *wake*."

In Lancashire, and particularly the south-eastern and eastern portions of the county, the wakes is the great holiday of the year. Though nominally commencing on the Sunday, it, in reality, began on the Saturday, on which day the rush-cart went round the neighbourhood, and lasted till Wednesday or Thursday in the following week. For some time previously work is steadily adhered to, in order that funds may be provided for the coming festival. The housewife cleans down the house (and a woman who does not do so at wakes time is looked upon by her neighbours as shirking her work), household treasures are brought forth, and displayed to the best advantage, the copper kettle, won at some local gooseberry-show, receives an extra polish, and the old grandsire's watch hung over the mantle-shelf, the wife's "grandmother's teapot" is displayed on the shelf against the wall, the pot church and dog ornaments on the mantle-shelf receive a good wash, and the chest of drawers, corner cupboard, and case-clock, get such a polish that they would serve as looking-glasses. Clean curtains are placed in the windows, and two or three pots of flowers, if not already there, brighten up the scene. The fire-grate is "blacked," and the floor—nearly always of flags in the country districts—scoured and sprinkled with sand. A batch of bread and oatcake is baked, pies and other dainties made, and often a brew takes place, if not of ale, then of nettles or some other herb, for the great impetus given to the increase of population in the manufacturing districts, has led to many seeking work and a home in the towns, and the wakes time affords an opportunity for revisiting relatives and friends in the country. Feasting and merrymaking take place, and in the evening these town-families may be seen returning home, laden with flowers, fruit, eggs, butter, fowls, and other country products. If the wakes is a noted one, strangers turn up in great numbers to see the rush-cart and morris-dancers, and generally to carouse with anyone likely to be "hail fellow, well met!" This unfortunately leads to drunkenness, brawls, and often riot.

The principal scene to be found at the wakes is on the green, or some open space as near the centre of the town or village as possible. Here gather a motley assemblage of fly-boats, merry-go-rounds, "dobby-horses," swing-boats, "Aunt Sallys," "knock-'em-downs," weighing-machines, "try-your-strength," and electric machines, shooting-galleries, and other devices for abstracting money from the pocket. The appetite is appealed to by booths for the sale of ginger-bread and sweet-cakes, especially made at some of these country wakes, bread and cheese, hot peas, toffy, "pop," and "ginger-beer," toys for the children, and nuts for all. In the larger towns these are increased by an occasional menagerie, a theatre—at which the performers make more show outside than in,—conjurers, marionettes, peep-shows, fat women and tall men, with monstrosities of various kinds. Occasionally a "cheap-jack" will be found palming off his rubbish on the gaping idler, whose dissatisfaction with his bargain merely serves to sharpen the wit of his companions. Here also may be seen the cart of the travelling photographer, who, for sixpence, turns out your likeness, ready framed, "while you wait."

Such are the sights which meet the eye. The sounds

which greet the ear are almost beyond description. Steam organs, steam whistles, hurdy-gurdies, drums, trumpets, gongs, rattles, men shouting, women screaming, children blowing penny-trumpets and crying, rifles popping, dogs barking—each trying to make itself heard above the rest—raise such a pandemonium that the quiet man who "does the wakes" stands a good chance of having a headache which will last him for days. The public-houses in the neighbourhood of the wakes ground do a roaring trade, and the passer-by hears a medley of singing and shouting, brawling and cursing, followed sometimes by an adjournment of the revellers to the pavement, in order to settle some drunken dispute. Towards evening, maudlin fellows may be seen led off home by their wives, the latter with their finery disarranged, their faces the colour of a peony, and tempers spoiled for a month at least.

In the outskirts dog-racing, and often dog-fighting, rabbit-coursing, pigeon-flying, running, leaping, wrestling, bicycle racing, and other sports, are provided. Formerly these sports were of a more brutal character, and the wakes without a bait of some kind was considered a farce. Bull-baiting was the one most in vogue, anyone being allowed to slip a dog on payment, generally, of a shilling. A well-trained dog ran under the bull's legs, and pinned it by the lips, the bull often raising the dog high in the air, and bringing it down with a whack on the ground in its pain. That dog was voted the best which pinned the bull in the neatest manner, and held on the longest. Young dogs, running straight at the bull, often met with severe treatment. Now and again the bull would break loose, and speedily clear the spot. In bear-baiting, the above tactics would not do, and a good dog at a bull would make but a poor show with a bear, who had to be pinned before he could use his claws. Badger-baiting

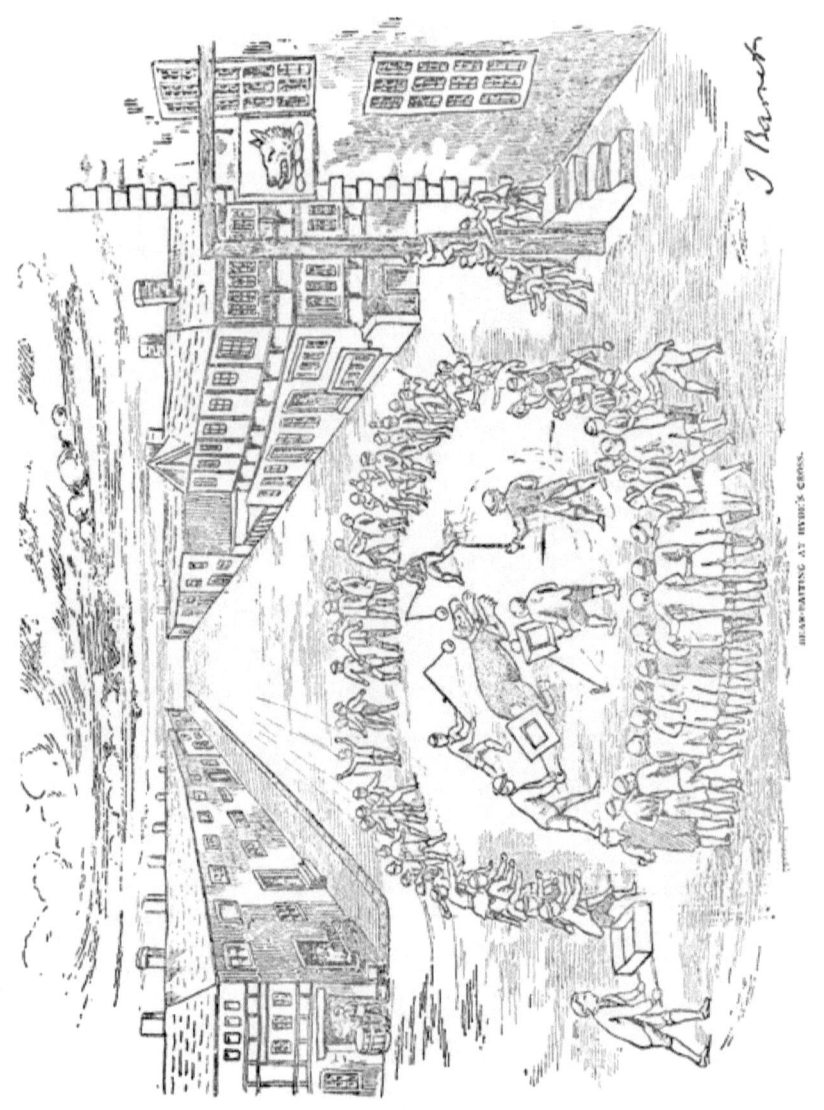

BEAR-BAITING AT HYDE'S CROSS.

also took place at many inns, the badger being placed, tail first, in a tub laid on the ground, so that he could only be met in front, and the dog had to lay hold and draw him out. Cock-fighting and dog-fighting were often eclipsed by a fight between two men in the old Lancashire style, stripped to the skin with the exception of a pair of clogs, striking, wrestling, " puncing," now up, now down, for the fight was continued on the ground until the vanquished one cried off. Shins presented a sorry sight, gashed in all directions by the kicks from the clogs, and for weeks after had to be carefully washed and bandaged. Yet these fierce encounters did not arise so often from hatred or a quarrel, but on slight provocation, as : " So-and-so is a better mon, and con feight thi." " Con he, by G—d, aw'll feight him," and the thing was done. The Lancashire lad was as ready for a fight as an Irishman, and several skits hit off this trait. Some little time after the resumption of work following a strike at Preston, a quaker shop-keeper called to his neighbour, " Hearsto, John, things are mendin', it's a lung time sin' aw saw a battle i' th' market-place, but aw've sin three this morning," and so accustomed were the wives to this fighting that it is related of one woman who went to fetch her " mon " from the wakes, and finding him disinclined to do so, asked him, " Was to foughten?" and receiving the reply, " neaw," told him to " get foughten, and come whoam."

The " Stockport Advertiser," of the 25th August, 1825, contains the following paragraph : " Didsbury wakes will be celebrated on the 8th, 9th, and 10th of August. A long bill of fare of the diversions to be enjoyed at this most delightful village has been published. The enjoyments consist chiefly of ass-races, for purses of gold ; prison-bar playing and grinning through collars, for ale ; bag-racing, for hats ; foot-racing, for sums of money ; maiden plates, for ladies under twenty years of age, for gown-pieces, shawls, etc.; treacled loaf-eating, for various rewards; smoking matches, apple dumpling-eating, wheelbarrow-racing, the best heats; bell-racing; and balls each evening. '*Quæ nunc præscribere longum est.*' The humours of Didsbury festival are always well-regulated, the display of youths of both sexes vieing with each other in dress and fashion, as well as cheerful and blooming faces, is not exceeded by any similar event, and the gaieties of each day are succeeded by the evening parties fantastically tripping through the innocent relaxation of country dances, reels, etc., to as favourite tunes, at the 'Cock' and 'Ring o' Bells' inns."

A singular wakes custom was introduced into Droylsden about 1814 from Woodhouses, where it had been prevalent for more than a third of a century. Chambers, in his "Edinburgh Journal" of November 19th, 1824, gives it a notice, as does also Bell, under the title of "The Greenside Wakes Song," in his annotated edition of the "English Poets."

The ceremonial issued from Greenside, and consisted of two male equestrians grotesquely habited. One, John, son of Robert Hulme, of Greenside, personified a man; the other, James, son of Aaron Etchells, of Edge-lane, a woman. They were engaged with spinning-wheels, spinning flax in the olden style, and conducting a rustic dialogue in limping verse, and gathering contributions from spectators. Latterly a cart was substituted for a saddle, as being a safer position in case they grew tipsy. Both Bell and Chambers translate the rhyme into "gradely English," and render Threedywheel *tread the wheel*, but it is evidently *thread the wheel*, as will be seen by a perusal of the original idiomatic and more spirited version :

"It's Dreighhodin wakes, un wey're commin to teawn,
To tell yo o' somethin' o' great reneawn,
Un iv this owd jade ull lemmi begin,
Aw'l show yo heaw hard un heaw fast aw con spin.

CHORUS.

So its threedywheel, threedywheel, dan, don, dill, doe.

Theaw brags o' thisel', bur aw dunno' think it true,
For aw will uphowd thi fawits arn't o few;
For when theaw hast done, un spun very hard,
O' this aw'm weel sure, thi work is ill marred.

CHORUS.

Theaw saucy owd jade theaudst best howd thi tung,
Or else awst be thumpin' thi ere it be lung;
Un iv ot aw do, theaust sure for to rue,
For aw con ha' monny o one as good as you.

CHORUS.

What is it to me whoe you can have?
Aw shanno be lung ere aw'm laid i' my grave;
Un when aw am deod yo may foind, iv yo con,
One ot'll spin is hard is aw've done.

CHORUS.

Com, com, mi dear woife, here endeth my sung,
Aw hope it has pleost this numerous thrung:
Bur iv it has mist, yo needn't to fear,
Wey'll do cawr endeavour to pleos um next year.

CHORUS.

So its threedywheel, threedywheel, dan, don, dill, doe." *

A hand-bill, of which the following is a copy, sets forth the programme of sports at the Eccles wakes of 1830:

"ECCLES WAKE.—On Monday morning, at eleven o'clock, the sports will commence with that most ancient, loyal, rational, constitutional, and lawful diversion,

BULL-BAITING,

in all its primitive excellence, for which this place has long been noted. At one o'clock there will be a foot-race; at two o'clock, a bull-baiting, for a horse-collar; at four, donkey-races, for a pair of pan-

* Higson's "History of Droylsden," 1859, pp. 65-66.

niers; at five, a race for a stuff hat; the day's sport to conclude with baiting the bull, 'Fury,' for a superior dog-chain. This animal is of gigantic strength and wonderful agility, and it is requested that the Fancy will bring their choice dogs on this occasion. The bull-ring will be stumped and railed round with English oak, so that

> The timid, the weak, the strong,
> The bold, the brave, the young,
> The old, friend, and stranger,
> Will be secure from danger.

"On Tuesday the sports will be repeated; also, on Wednesday, with the additional attraction of a smock-race by ladies. A main of cocks to be fought on Monday, Tuesday, and Wednesday, for twenty guineas, and five guineas the byes, between the gentlemen of Manchester and Eccles. The wake to conclude with a fiddling-match, by all the fiddlers that attend, for a piece of silver."

At the wakes held 2nd September, 1833, a swing-boat broke down with seven or eight children in it, and one girl was killed. During the baiting of the bull several cows passed near to the ring, and whilst winding their way through the crowd, a bull-dog suddenly sprang on one of them, which caused the affrighted animal to overturn a cart of nuts, and a girl had her leg broken in consequence.

Eccles was long celebrated for its wakes and its cakes, but the former has almost died out. Bull and bear-baiting ceased in 1834. The bull used to be baited on the south side of a plot of vacant land at the Regent Road entrance to the village. At the last bull-bait, a stand erected for the use of spectators fell, and several people were injured. One of them, a woman, died some little time after. The last bull that was baited in Eccles was taken to Chowbent, and as it was led out of Eccles it was bestridden by a fiddler and a trumpeter, both of whom played on their respective instruments. The ring, fastened to a post sunk into the ground, remained for some time after. The bears used to be baited on the south side of a plot of waste ground near the "Cross Keys Hotel."*

* "Manchester Guardian."—Notes and Queries, No. 1192.

A picture of Eccles Wakes was painted by Joseph Parry, R.S.A., of Manchester, in 1822, for the late Mr. Thomas Kaye, publisher and editor of the "Liverpool Courier." Like Thompson, in his picture of the Rush-bearing at Borrowdale, the artist has drawn freely on his imagination, and the scene is quite unlike the village of Eccles. The picture is thirty-five inches long, and twenty-four inches wide, containing not less than 200 figures. In the background is a church, with large masses of foliage, intermixed with which are several old-fashioned tenements, conspicuous among them standing "The Old Original Red Lion." On the extreme left are depicted a bull-bait and the prize ring, while combats with single-stick are going on in various parts of the ground. In the centre are a train of morris-dancers, a sweep assuming the character of "Flibbertigibbet," the tomfool of the village, and other amusing characters in grotesque costumes. A genteel group occupies the centre of the foreground; the papa and the children are enjoying the fun very much, while the lady turns up her nose at the disorderly scenes. On the right, a vendor of the far-famed Eccles cakes plying his trade, two devoted worshippers of Bacchus, a lad on an ass, and some domestic scenes form a motley group.*

A small pamphlet, without date, was published, entitled: "The Country Wakes: A Critique upon a Picture of Eccles Wakes, painted by Parry, of Manchester," 1822, 12mo., 15 pp.

In Westhoughton, at the annual feast or wakes, there is a singular local custom of making large flat pasties of pork, which are eaten in great quantities on the Wakes Sunday, with a liberal accompaniment of ale; and people resort to the village from all places for miles round, on this Sunday, just as they rush into Bury on Mid-Lent or Mothering Sunday to eat simnels and

* "Manchester Guardian."—Notes and Queries, No. 974.

drink bragot ale. On the completion of the wakes in August, 1890, a peculiar procession took place, in which the members of the "Bone Club" took part. The leaders carried broom-handles, upon which were placed skeletons of cows' heads, decorated with ribbons, and others carried jaw-bones. The music was provided with tin whistles. Copious refreshments were provided at public-houses.

The Rush.

"Can the rush grow up without mire? can the flag grow without water?"
— JOB, viii., 2.

HE rush, "trodden under foot," was considered of so little value as to give rise to the saying, "not worth a rush," in which sense it is used by Gower:

"For til I se the daie springe,
I sette slepe *nought at a rushe.*"

Other instances occur, as:

"*Not worth a rush*, master, whether apes go on four legs or two."
L'Estrange.

"But hee not pinned alwayes on her sleeves; strangers have greene rushes, when daily guests are *not worth a rush.*" Lyly's "Sapho and Phaon," ii., 4.

And

"John Bull's friendship is *not worth a rush.*"—Arbuthnot.

Skelton also makes use of the same term, yet, like many other of our old sayings, it requires some modification. The pith of the rush formed a cheap and easily-obtained wick for the "rush-light;" the rush supplied the only carpet or covering for the rude floors of our ancestors for centuries; the "hassock" on which he knelt; mats, which sold at from 6d. to several shillings, on which he cleaned his shoes; seats for his chairs; ropes for several purposes; toys for his children; a charm for the cure of disease; and, formed into a ring, was used for the purpose of deluding ignorant and immoral females into a mock marriage. Baskets were made of rushes in the earliest times. They were also used for wrapping in them concrete milk (? cheese). An instrument to catch fish was also made of them. Rolls to stuff capes of robes were made of the pith. There were particular trades who worked in them. The species *Scirpus* was manufactured into hats, mats, thatch for houses, sails of ships, etc. The *pith*, covered with wax, was the wick of torches. It was also termed the *papyrus*, and the interior laminæ might be used for a fine paper. *

Rushes were also used for beds. An eighteenth century ballad says:

> "Fair Lady, rest till morning blushes,
> I'll strew for thee a *bed of rushes.*"
> —*Oh! Lady Fair.*

And in the first part of "Henry IV.," iii., 1:

> "She bids you
> Upon the wanton rushes lay you down."

Goldsmith also mentions this use of the rush:

> "My *rushy couch* and frugal fare."

The rush is frequently mentioned by the old writers:

> "Man but a *rush* against Othello's breast,
> And he retires."
> —*Shakspeare, "Othello."*

> "Your farm requites your pains;
> Though *rushes* overspread the neighb'ring plains."
> —*Dryden.*

> "In *rushy* grounds, springs are found at the first spit."—*Mortimer.*

> "The timid hare to some lone seat
> Retir'd; the *rushy* fen or rugged furze."
> —*Thomson.*

In Lancashire, "hassock" is a reed, rush, or coarse grass (such as "scuch" or "couch" grass), formerly used for making mats; hence the term is applied to

---

* See Fosbrooke's "Encyclopædia of Antiquities," 1843, vol. 1, p. 509.

mats, and to the cushions, or "stools," on which people kneel at church:

"1729, July 1. Set my son John to lead [cart] *hassocks* to Longridge."—*Walkden's Diary.*

Stacks, barns, outhouses, and cottages were often covered with sods instead of thatch. The coarse grass and rushes from the top of a moss was much used for this purpose. Again quoting Walkden, under date 7th July, 1729:

"So wanting some hassock turf to top our stack with . . . son John led me 4 double loads home, and 2 double loads to John Bleasdale's for John Bleasdale, at 3d. per load." "July 8. In the afternoon, finished my stacking." "July 9. . . . I sodded the turf stack top."

A Scotch ballad tells us how Bessie Bell and Mary Gray:

"They biggèd a bower on yon burn brae,
And *theekit* it ower wi' *rashes*."

Twisted into ropes, the rush was used for securing thatched roofs, and for trussing hay and straw, being more pliant and stronger than ropes made of straw.

The accompanying figure of an Italian rush-gatherer, from a drawing by E. Cecconi, is taken from the "Art Journal," 1885, p. 375.

The word *juncare*—meaning to strew with rushes—is sometimes used in the West of England, when referring to the custom of strewing rushes, evidently derived from the Latin *juncus*, a bulrush. Du Cange gives, "*Juncare*, spargere flores." *Jonciere* is a bed of rushes; *juncous*, full of rushes.—(Ash's "Dictionary," 1779). *Juncare* (old Latin), to strew with rushes, according to the old custom of adorning churches.—(Bailey's "Dictionary," 1789). *Joncher*, to strew, to spread, or cover (as) with rushes. (Cotgrave).

Rush-bearings have been absurdly attributed, in their origin, to an anonymous festival, in which the Pagans expressed their unity and concord by rushes. "I was

THE RUSH GATHERER.

led to this," says Ebenezer Hunt, "by examining the Latin *Juncus*, a Rush, which both Rider and Littleton derive 'a Jungendo, quoniam ejus usus ad juncturas utilis; vel quod junctis radicibus hæreat,' from joining, because it was used for binding things, or because it joins together in the roots, it being the custom formerly to make ropes of them, and which, in some measure, obtains among country people in our day; and the roots, adhering together in their growth, will bear the latter sense; either of which is farther confirmed by its German name, Binz, from *binden*, to bind.—*Vide* Parkhurst's 'Greek Lexicon,' under Schoinion." *

Dr. Bullein,† who speaks much in general commendation of the rush for its utility, informs us that "rushes that grow upon dry grounds be good to strew in halles, chambers, and galleries, to walke upon, *defending apparrell as traynes of gownes and kertles from dust*. Rushes be olde courtiers, and when they be nothing worth then they be cast out of the doores; so be many that do treade upon them."

In Somersetshire, the name of bulrush is applied to the common rush (*Juncus*), "and this is quite intelligible, if we understand the name to be the same as Pole-rush or Pool-rush, which is said to be found in old writers. This was given to the plant from its growing in pools, like the French *Jone d'eau*, and the Anglo-Saxon *Ea-risce*, only that the Scirpus is to be understood in these cases." ‡

The "rush" in most frequent use was probably the *Acorus calamus*, or sweet flag, which though, botanically speaking, not a rush at all, would be thus loosely classed by a rustic gatherer.

RUSH-CHAIRS.—"The use of rush-bottomed chairs," says Tuer, § "which are again coming into æsthetic

* Hampson's "Medii Ævi Kalendarium," 1841, p. 343.
† "Bulwarke of Defence," 1579, fol. 21.
‡ Friend's "Flowers and Flower Lore," 1886, p. 475.
§ "Old London Street Cries," 1885, p. 108.

"CHAIRS TO MEND!"

fashion, cannot be traced back quite a century and a half." The chairs in the time of Elizabeth were wood, with the seats and backs stuffed. In that of Queen Anne, they were seated and backed with cane. In the country districts the cry of "chairs to mend" is frequently heard, the stock-in-trade of the travelling chair-mender consisting of a thick bundle of pliant dried rushes, generally six feet long, and a few tools, and, in some cases, a smaller bundle of split canes. The charge for re-bottoming a chair runs from 1s. 6d. to 2s. 6d., and they are more comfortable to sit upon than cane ones.

RUSH-CHARMS.—In Devonshire, the rush is used in a charm for the thrush, as follows: Take three rushes from any running stream, and pass them separately through the mouth of the infant, then plunge the rushes again into the stream, and as the current bears them away, so will the thrush depart from the child.

In Cheshire, rushes are used as a charm for warts. I have several times seen an old man proceed as follows: Taking a long, straight rush, he tied three knots on it, then, making it into a circle, he drew it over the wart downwards nine times, at the same time mumbling something (which he stoutly refused to divulge, on the plea that if he did the cure would not work). The wart would disappear in three months, unconsciously. I have met several people who firmly believe in its efficacy. It seems that the secret was told him on the express injunction that he should only impart it to one other person, with a similar injunction, in his lifetime, otherwise he would lose the gift.

To find a four-leaved clover, a double-leaved ash, and a green-topped rush was deemed very lucky:

"With a four-leaved Clover, a double-leaved Ash, and green-topped Seave,
You may go before the queen's daughter without asking leave."

RUSH-FUZES.—The Cornish miners formerly used

rushes for fuzes, the pith being taken out and then filled with gunpowder. A prepared fuze of paper, or match, was affixed to the top of the rush, of a length sufficient to permit the miner to get out of the way of the explosion.

RUSH-LIGHTS, or candles with rush wicks, are of the greatest antiquity, for we learn from Pliny that the Romans applied different kinds of rushes to a similar purpose, as making them into flambeaux and wax-candles for use at funerals. The earliest Irish candles were rushes dipped in grease and placed in lamps of oil, and they have been similarly used in many districts of England. In Baret's "Alvearie," fol., London, 1580, R. 481, "The rush, weeke, or match that mainteineth the light in the lampe" is spoken of. Aubrey, writing about 1673, says that he saw at Ockley, in Surrey, "the people draw peeled rushes through melted grease, which yields a sufficient light for ordinary use, is very cheap and useful, and burnes long." *

The Rev. Gilbert White has devoted one letter in his interesting work † to this simple piece of domestic economy. He tells us :

"The proper species is the common soft rush, found in most pastures by the sides of streams and under hedges. Decayed labourers, women, and children gather these rushes late in summer. As soon as they are cut, they must be flung into water, and kept there, otherwise they will dry and shrink, and the peel will not run. When peeled they must lie on the grass to be bleached, and take the dew for some nights, after which they are dried in the sun. Some address is required in dipping these rushes into the scalding fat or grease. The careful wife of an industrious Hampshire labourer obtains all her fat for nothing, for she saves the scummings of her bacon pot for this use; and if the grease abound with salt she causes the salt to precipitate to the bottom, by setting the scummings in a warm oven. Where hogs are not much in use, and especially by the seaside, the coarse animal oils will come very cheap. A pound of common grease may be procured for fourpence, and about six pounds of grease will dip a pound of rushes, which cost one shilling, so that a

* Chambers's "Book of Days," 1863, vol. I, p. 507.
† "Natural History of Selborne."

pound of rushes, ready for burning, will cost three shillings. If men that keep bees will mix a little wax with the grease, it will give it a consistency, and render it more cleanly, and make the rushes burn longer, mutton suet will have the same effect.

"A pound avoirdupois contains 1600 rushes; and supposing each to burn on an average but half-an-hour, then a poor man will purchase 800 hours of light, a time exceeding thirty-three entire days, for three shillings. According to this account, each rush, before dipping, costs one thirty-third of a farthing, and one-eleventh afterwards. Thus a poor family will enjoy five-and-a-half hours of comfortable light for a farthing. An experienced old housekeeper assured Mr. White that one pound and a half of rushes completely supplied her family the year round, since working people burn no candle in the long days, because they rise and go to bed by daylight.

"Little farmers use rushes in the short days both morning and evening, in the dairy and kitchen; but the very poor, who are always the worst economists, and therefore must continue very poor, buy a halfpenny candle every evening, which, in their blowing, open rooms, does not burn much longer than two hours. Thus, they have only two hours' light for their money, instead of eleven."

Rush-lights were, however, not peculiar to the southern part of the country:

"In the fall of the year, a caller at any Seathwaite farmhouse will notice upon a hanging shelf, or some such repository, a bundle of what looks rather like dirty straw, but which, on examination, turns out to be half-peeled rushes saturated with fat, and are the principal, if not the sole provision made for the supply of light to the household in the evenings of winter. In the dales around Seathwaite, a proverbial saying may be heard to the effect that a 'Seathwaite candle's a greased seeve,' seeve being Cumbrian for rush." *

I remember these rush-lights in Cheshire, within the last twenty years, being sold twenty for sixpence. They were as thick as the present "twelves" candles (twelve to the pound), but half as long again, and gave a steady but dim light. There were some curious bits of folk lore connected with them; for instance, if a rush-light in "swealing" curled over, it denoted death; if a bright star appeared in the flame it portended a letter. One old woman used to make her own lights, in a somewhat similar manner to that related by Gilbert

---

* Harland and Wilkinson's "Lancashire Legends," etc., 1873, p. 204.

White, gathering the long pliant rushes growing in very wet places, and dressing them by the side of a pond, wetting them several times a day in the manner thatchers do with straw for thatching. When sufficiently cured, she peeled them (the pith alone being used). The grease was "dripping," which she got from her better-provided neighbours, and mixed with it a little mutton fat, boiling it in a large pan on the fire. Then, taking several rush piths, and tying one end to a stick with thread, so that they hung down, she dipped them into the pot, which stood on the "hob" to keep the grease warm, afterwards hanging the stick on something to cool, whilst she went on with another lot, alternately dipping and cooling till they were thick enough to her liking.

A writer describes them as "a small blinking taper, made by stripping a rush, except one small stripe of the bark which holds the pith together, and dipping it in tallow." When used as night-lights, the length of time they were required to burn was regulated by thrusting two pins through the pith, on burning down to which the light went out.

A "rush-holder" was used in burning them, specimens of which are given on next page. Figure 1 is an ordinary rush-holder, from Chambers's "Book of Days;" figure 2 shows specimens of Sussex iron rush-light and dip-holders in the collection of Lady Dorothy Nevill, taken from the "Art Journal" (1886, pp. 372-3); *a* is an early form of rush-holder, the spring clip for the rush is inserted in the stand, the whole is a foot high; *b* is a rush-light and dip-holder combined, with rack stand for altering the height of light, it is about three feet high; *c* is a rush and dip-holder; *d* is a rush-light and holder stand; the candlestick is gone in this example, but the dotted lines give its place; in the opinion of Lady Dorothy Nevill it was a votive candle for a church; *e* rush-holder and candlestick, this, in her

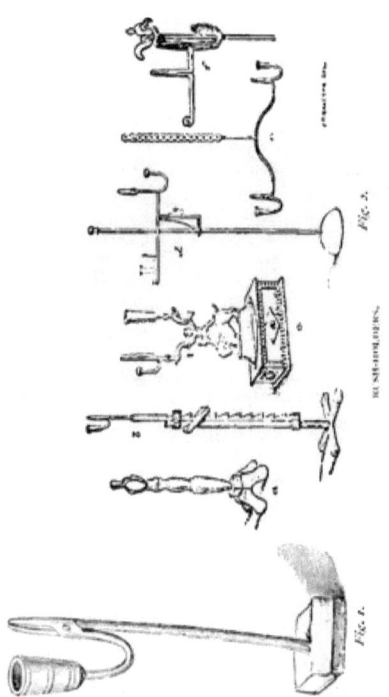

ladyship's opinion, was suspended in the roomy old fire-place; *f* is the top only of a stand rush-holder, drawn on a larger scale; here the artist in iron has ornamented the top with a rude resemblance of a cock. The stand itself is about four feet high, and the light can be raised or lowered when required.

Shakspeare alludes to the rush-candle:

> "Be it moon or sun, or what you please:
> And if you please to call it a *rush-candle*,
> Henceforth it shall be so to me."

And Milton:

> "If your influence be quite dam'd up
> With black usurping mists, some gentle taper,
> Though a *rush-candle* from the wicker hole
> Of some clay habitation, visit us."

A Lancashire "saying" says of a sprightly youth:

> "His een twinkle like a *farthing rush-light.*"

RUSH-RINGS.—A passage in Shakspeare's "All's Well that Ends Well," Act ii., Scene 2:

> "As Tib's rush for Tom's forefinger,"

which long puzzled commentators, led Douce* to write a learned note on the subject, which is worth reproducing. He says:

> "The covert allusion mentioned by Mr. Ritson is, in all probability, the right solution of this passage: but the practice of marrying with a rush-ring may admit of some additional remarks. Sir John Hawkins had already, in a very curious and interesting note, illustrated the subject; and it must appear very extraordinary that *one of the subsequent notes* should question the practice of marrying with a rush-ring, on the grounds that *no authority* had been produced in support of it. This must therefore be explained. The fact is that the author of the doubts had never seen Sir John Hawkins' *entire note*, which had originally appeared in the edition of 1778, but was injudiciously suppressed in that of 1785. In the edition of 1790, there is only a

---

* "Illustrations of Shakspeare, and of Ancient Manners," 1839, pp. 194-196.

brief and general statement of Sir John's opinion, and this led to the doubts expressed. In 1793, Mr. Steevens restores a note which he had already cancelled, and, with all its authorities before him, permits them to be questioned; but there are many who will comprehend his motive.

"The information from De Breul (not Breval, as misprinted), 'Theatre des antiquitez de Paris,' 1612, 4to., is worth stating more at large. The author tells us that in the official court of the church of Saint Marinus, those who had lived unchastely are conducted to the church by two officers, in case they refuse to go of their own accord, and there married by the curate with a *rush-ring*. They are likewise enjoined to live in peace and friendship, thereby to preserve the honour of their friends and relations, and their own souls from the danger they had incurred. This is only practised where no method of saving the honour of the parties and their connexions can be devised. A modern French writer remarks on this ceremony, 'pour faire observer, sans doute, au mari, combien etoit *fragile la vertu* de celle qu'il choisis sait.'

"With respect to the constitution of the bishop of Salisbury in 1217, which forbid the putting of *rush-rings* on women's fingers, there seems to be an *error* in the reason for this prohibition as stated by Sir John Hawkins, but for which he is not perhaps responsible. He says it is insinuated by the bishop 'that there were some people weak enough to believe that what was thus done in jest, was a real marriage.' The original words, as in Spelman's 'Councils,' are these: 'ne dum jocari se putat, honoribus matrimonialibus se *abstringat*.' Now, unless we read '*adstringat*,' there is a difficulty in making sense of the passage, which seems to mean, '*least, whilst he thinks he is only practising a joke, he may be tying himself in the matrimonial noose.*' It is to be observed that this consequence was not limited to the deception of putting a rush-ring on the woman's finger, but any ring whatever, whether of vile or of precious materials."

In Green's "Menaphon" is this passage: "Well, 'twas a good worlde when such simplicitie was used, sayes the old women of our time, when a *ring of a rush* would tie as much love together as a gimmon of golde." But *rush-rings* were sometimes innocently used. Thus in Spencer's "Shepherd's Calendar," 1579, 4to., Ægloga xi. :

"*Colin:* 'Where be the nosegays that she dight for thee?
The colour'd chapelets wrought with a chief,
The *knotted rush-rings*, and gilt rosemary?
For she deemed no thing too dear for thee.'"

In D'Avenant's "Rivals," also:

> "I'll crown thee with a garland of straw, then,
> And I'll marry thee with a *rush-ring*."

Again, in Fletcher's "Two Noble Kinsmen," Act iv.:

> ". . . . . *Rings* she made
> Of *rushes* that grew by, and to 'em spoke
> The prettiest poesies: thus our true love's ty'd;
> This you may lose, not me; and many a one."

> "And Tommy was so to Katty,
> And wedded her with a *rush-ring*."
> —*Winchest. Wedding Pills to Purge, Med., vol. i., p. 276.*

Brand* says: "A custom extremely hurtful to the interests of morality, appears anciently to have prevailed both in England and other countries, of marrying with a *Rush-Ring*. It was chiefly practised, however, by designing men, for the purpose of debauching their mistresses, who sometimes were so infatuated as to believe that this mock ceremony was a real marriage."

Shakspeare, speaking of love, says:

> "He taught me how to know a man in love; in which cage of *rushes* I am sure you are not a prisoner."

RUSH-ROPES.—Ropes, stronger and more durable than of hemp, are said to have been made of rushes. Plot † was shown at Park Hall, in the parish of Caverswall, "a rope that past between the runners of the oat-mill . . . made only of the pillings or rinds pull'd off the pith of the juncus lævis panicula sparsa major, or juncus lævis vulgaris, both of which it seems are Candle rushes, which, they told me, would not only last a year, *i.e.*, longer than one of hemp, but that it would not stretch as hempen ones do, which, it seems, is a great convenience in the working of such a mill."

---
* "Popular Antiquities," edition 1877, p. 359.
† "Natural History of Staffordshire," 1686, p. 379.

Westmacott, whose "Historia Vegetabilium Sacra; or, A Scripture Herbal," was published in 1694, eight years only after Plot's work, speaks of the same rope in almost identical words: "A rarity not far off me, at Park Hall, is a rope that passes between the runners of the oat-mill, made only of the peelings or rinds of candle-rushes, *juncus lævis vulgaris*, which doth not only last longer than one of hemp, but will not stretch as hempen ones do, which is a great convenience in the working of such kind of mills. The moss-rush, *Juncus acutus Cambro Britannicus*, is called goosecorns. Bull-rushes, in some counties, are called bumbles."

At the present time, rush-ropes are made by Messrs. James Evans & Co., Gaythorn, Manchester, for use as cores in iron foundries, and for packing purposes.

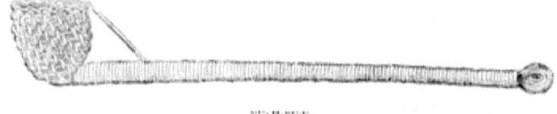

RUSH-PIPE.

They are spun on a machine, and are of uniform thickness throughout, free from knots, are very strong, and do not unwind on being cut. They are made in lengths of about 200 yards, and the price per 1000 yards is about: No. 1 (thick), 17s. 6d.; No. 2 (medium), 11s.; No. 3 (thin), 8s. 6d. The rush-ropes are much preferred to straw-ropes, and are mostly used for cylinders and special kinds of work, and where a particularly true core is required.

RUSH-TOYS.—Children plait and bind rushes into a variety of toys, as whips, pipes, miniature chairs, baskets, caps, harps, etc. In the autumn, rush-pipes are frequently sold in the streets at a penny each, the stem about two feet long, and the bowl three-and-a-half inches in diameter. Bulrushes are also sold at three a penny.

Wright ("Dictionary of Obsolete and Provincial English," 1869) gives:

"RUSHY-MILS.—A sportive imitation of mills, made by the shepherds in running water, and composed of rushes."

> "His spring should flow some other way; no more
> Should it in wanton manner ere be seene
> To writhe in knots, or give a gown of greene
> Unto their meadowes; nor be seene to play,
> Nor drive the *rushy-mils*, that in his way
> The shepherd made."
>
> *Brown,* "*British Pastimes,*" *I., i., v. 722.*

Shakspeare, "Coriolanus," i., 4, says:

> "Our gates,
> Which yet seem shut, we have but pinned with rushes;
> They'll open of themselves."

The word rush bears several meanings, as:

RUSH (*s.*) —A merry-making.
    A patch of underwood.
    A disease in cattle.
RUSH-BEARING (*s.*)— The day of a church's dedication.
    "Another name for the parish wakes, held at the feast of the dedication of each church, when the parishioners brought fresh rushes to strew the church."—*Nare's* "*Glossary,*" *1888, p. 756.*
RUSH-BUCKLER (*s*) —A swash-buckler.
    "Take into this number also their servants; I mean all that flock of stout, bragging *rush-bucklers*" "*More's Utopia,*" *by R. Robinson, vol. 2, p. 39, Dibdin.*
RUSHE (*v.*)— To dash down.
RUSHEWS, OR RISHEWS (*s*)— An article of confectionery.
RUSHIN (*s.*) A tub of butter.
RUSHING (*s.*) —Refreshment.
RISH (*s.*) A rush.
    (*v*)— To gather rushes.
    (*s*)—A sickle.
    (*adv.*) Directly, quickly.
RISHUNDRY (*s.*)— Loose corn left in the field, and become so dry as to be rather brittle.

"What knight like him could toss the rushy lance."
Tickel.

William Andrews & Co., The Hull Press.

Index

Abingdon, Mayor's Sunday at, 6
Aylesbury tenure, 1

Bear-baits, 59, 158
Benefactions at
    Bristol, 23
    Deptford, 21
    Glenfield, 22
    Middleton, 23
    Old Weston, 22
    South Cerney, 23
    Tatton, 22
    Wingrave, 21
Blacks and Jacks, riot, 66
Bone club, a, 165
Bull-baits, 76, 158

Churches, rush-strewing in, 13
    Rush-carrying to, 24
    Characters at, 28
    Dixon, Rev. J., poem by, 29
    Donnington, 28
    Hone's Year Book quoted, 36
    Lake district, 29
    Lloyd, Rev. Owen, hymn by, 36
    Marton, 38
    Origin of, Notes on, 25-27
    "The Queen" quoted, 34
    Thompson, Jacob, picture by, 29
    Winter, Miss, sketch by, 36
Contumacious Robert Aughton, 16

Dancing, 9

Easter Day Customs, 7

Frumenty, 155

Garlands in Churches, 89
    Castleton, 91
    Droylesden, 93
    Redcliff, 90

"Going to sweeten," 7
Graves, decorating, 76
Greenside wakes' song, the, 162

Houses, rush-strewing in, 1

Juncate, 168

Kemp's nine days' wonder
    Incident at, 131
    At Chelmsford, 133
    At Sudbury, 134
King, rushes for the, 2

Lancashire pugnacity, 160
Liskeard, recent use of rushes at, 11
London, regulations at, 2
"Longwood Thump," 81

Manchester, Alexander Wilson's picture, 63
May-Day custom, a, 11
Morris-dance, the, 95
    Baxter, Richard, on the, 109
    Betley, window at, 102
    At Christmas, 118
    Churchwardens' accounts, 104
    At Clerkenwell, 114
    Cobbe's account, 110
    On Corpus Christi day, 97
    In Cripplegate, 106
    Dancers, 95
    In Derbyshire, 115
    Douce's remarks, 197
    Dress, 121-28
    Harleian MS., 111
    In Lancashire, 117
    Salt, 111
    Officers, 139
    Speech, 143
    Munich, carving at, 102
    In Northamptonshire, 115, 119

Morris-dance —
  At Northenden, 115
  In Oxfordshire, 114
  Petrarch coronation, 97
  Puritan diatribes, 109
  At Reading, 106
  The restoration, 112
  Van Mecheln's engraving, 97
  Vendome, 96
  Vinckenboom's painting, 104
Murder, incident of, 10

Old Meg of Herefordshire, etc., 135-142

Processions, 6

Remarkable customs, M. Daudelot, 4
Restoration ceremonies, 78
Riot at Gorton, 60
Royal residences, etc., 3
Rush-bearing, Jesse Lee's description, 68
Rush, the, 166
  Chairs, 170
  Charms, 172
  Holders, 175
  Lights, 173
  Many uses of, 166-70
  Mills, Rushy, 181
  " Not worth a," 4, 166
  Rings, 177
  Ropes, 179
  Toys, 180
Rush-cart, the, 24, 39
  At Burnedge, 80
  At Banbury, 75
  At Chapel-en-le-Frith, 78
  At Dent, 78
 Described by (or in)
  Bamford's early days, 42
  Sir J. P. Kay-Shuttleworth, 49
  Frances Ann Kemble, 48
  Lancashire legends, 40
  Lancashire memories, 48
  Pictorial history of Lancashire, 51
  Elijah Ridings, 39
  Roby, 40
  At Didsbury, 55
  At Droylesden, 56
  At Forest Chapel, 77
  At Gorton, 57
  Higson, John, 57
  At Lynn, 75
  At Manchester (visit), 63
  At Milnrow, 73
  At Newton Heath, 55
  A riot, 71

Rush-cart
  At Rochdale, 65
  At Runcorn, 76
  Saddleworth, 79
  Uppermill, 81
  At Whalley, 73
  At Wilmslow, 77
Rush-cutting, right of, at Clee, 21
Rushy Mills, 181
Rush-strewing in churches, 13
  At Bristol, 20
  At Castleton, 14
  At Habsham, 20
  At Hardley, 20
  At Heybridge, 14
  At Kirkham, 14
  At Norwich, 20
  At Pilling, 14
  At Salisbury, 13
Skedlock-carts, 55
Stage, the, 11
St. Oswald's Church, Chester, 13

Tenures, 1
Town and churchwarden's accounts, etc., 17
Trinity House, Hull, etc., 11

Unseemly customs, 8

Vigils, see Wakes, 147

Wakes, 14
  Charles I., 153
  At Didsbury, 160
  At Disley, 14
  At Droylesden, 161
  At Eccles, 162
  At Gorton, 14
  In Lancashire, 152
  At Manchester, 151
  At Newton, 16
 Quotations
  Hinde and others, against, 154
  Dr. Jayne, in favour, 155
  Ben Johnson, 152
  Old Writer v. Strutt, 148
  Pope Gregory, 149
  Stubbs, 152
  At Stockport, 14
  Suppressed, 150
  At Westhoughton, 163
Whitlers, 140
Whitsun-ale, 119

York, priestly processions, 7

List of Subscribers.

Alexander, J. Fletcher, 36, St. Peter's Street, Ipswich.
Alexander, Joseph E. W., Sunnyside, Lansdowne Road, Didsbury.
Alexander, Joseph J., 76, King Street, Manchester.
Allsopp, Hon. A. P., M.P.
Andrews, William, F.R.H.S., 1, Dock Street, Hull (2 copies).
Armstrong, Edgar, 7, Wycliffe Road, Urmston, Manchester.
Armstrong, George B., 88, Deansgate, Manchester.
Armstrong, Thomas, Brookfield, Urmston.
Arnold, Clarence, St. Ann's Square, Manchester.
Allen, Edward G., 28, Henrietta Street, Covent Garden, London, W.
Andrade, Benjamin, 26, Somerleyton Road, Brixton, S.W.
Armytage, Capt. Godfrey, The Court, Ackworth, Pontefract.
Armytage, George T., F.S.A., Clifton Woodhead, Brighouse.
Atkinson, Miss C., Moor Allerton Lodge, Leeds.
Atkinson, Rev. Dr., Clare College Lodge, Cambridge.

Beauchamp, The Earl, 13, Belgrave Square, London, S.W. (2 copies).
Brooke, Alexander, Handford, Cheshire (2 copies).
Bennett, Edgar, Court Ash, Yeovil.
Brammall, John Holland, Sale Hill House, Sheffield.
Briggs, A., Rawden Hall, near Leeds.
Brent, Cecil, F.S.A., 37, Palace Grove, Bromley, Kent.
Brown-Dixon, D., Unthank Hall, Haltwhistle, Carlisle.
Britton, Albert, 5, Talford Grove, Albert Park, Didsbury.
Bell, Mackenzie, Elmstead, Carlton Road, Putney, S.W.
Binns, J. Arthur, Bradford, Yorkshire.
Brushfield, T. N., M.D., The Cliff, Budleigh Salterton, Devonshire.
Buxton, J. H., Clumber House, Poynton, near Stockport.
Brittain, Ald. W. H., J.P., F.R.H.S., Storth Oaks, Sheffield.
Beverley, W. H., M.R.C.S., 13, Albion Road, South Cliff, Scarboro'.
Bethell, William, North Grimstone House, York.
Bancroft, W., Solicitor, Northwich.
Banks, W., 42, Lime Street, Riston.
Bailey, Ald. William H., Albion Works, Salford.
Bostock, R. C., Tarporley, Thurlestone Road, West Norwood, S.E.
Beck, Rev. James, F.S.A., Bildeston Rectory, Suffolk.
Bullen, A. H., 1, Yelverton Villas, Twickenham.

Crane, Walter, Beaumont Lodge, Shepherd's Bush, W.
Caswell, C. J., Horncastle.
Carter, F. R., Savile House, Potter Newton, Leeds.
Cliff, John, F.R.H.S., Fulneck, Leeds.
Camidge, Wm., 36, Monkgate, York.

2C

Cordingley, John R., 10, Melbourne Place, Bradford.
Cummings, Wm. H., f.s.a., Sydcote, West Dulwich, S.E.
Clayton, Thos. F., Cheadle Hulme.
Clayton, T. C., Starkie House, Adlington, near Macclesfield.
Charlesworth, Rev. E. G., Acklam Vicarage, Middlesborough-on-Tees.
Cowie, Very Rev. B. M., Dean of Exeter, The Deanery, Exeter.
Creek, Mrs., Victoria Terrace, Cheadle Hulme.
Chambers, Edmund K., Corpus Christi College, Oxford.
Colman, J. J., m.p., Carrow House, Norwich.
Cook, Jas. Wm., Wentworth House, Hollybush Hill, Snaresbrook, Essex.
Chadburn, William, The Lodge, Bramhall Hall, Stockport.
Cambridge Free Library, per J. Pink, Librarian.
Carington, H. H. Smith, Stanley Grove, Oxford Road, Manchester.

Dalzell, Thos. Henry, j.p., Clifton Hall, Workington, Cumberland.
Dearden, John K., Leahurst, 25, Lansdowne Road, Didsbury.
Dennis, Cammack, Rochdale Road, Bury, Lancs.
Davenport, G., Brow Hill, Leek.
Davenport, H., Woodcroft, Leek.
Diggles, Alfred S., Bramhall, Stockport.
Davis, John, Bifrons, Farnboro', Hants.

Eagle, William, 77, King Street, Manchester.
Eastwood, J. A., 49, Princess Street, Manchester.
Eccles, Wm. E., Moorfield House, Rishton, Blackburn.
Elvin, Chas. Norton, m.a., Eckling Grange, East Dereham, Norfolk.
Entwisle, Thomas, 60, Adswood Lane East, Stockport.
Embleton, D., m.d., 19, Claremont Place, Newcastle-upon-Tyne.
Embleton Thos. W., The Cedars, Methey, Lewes.
Evans, Dr. John, Nash Mills, Hemel Hempstead.

Farrah, John, Low Harrogate.
Feather, Rev. G., Glazebury Vicarage, near Manchester.
Fenton, Jas., m.a., f.s.a., j.p., Barrister-at-Law, Dutton Manor, Longridge, near Preston, Lancs.
Formby, Jonathan, Barrister-at-Law, The Firs, Formby, near Liverpool.
Foljambe, Cecil G. S., m.p., Cockglode, Ollerton, Newark.
Firth, Solomon, f.r.h.s., 24, Alton Villas, Highfields, Leicester.
Free Public Library, Heywood, per J. Leach, Librarian.
Free Public Library, St. Helens, Lancs., per A. Lancaster.
Falkner, Robt., 176, Deansgate, Manchester.
Fitton, Hedley, 76, Northen Grove, Didsbury.
Fraser, Thomas, 94, High Street, Dalbeattie, N.B.
Foster, H. G., 15, Aberdeen Park, Highbury, London, N.

Gabb, Rev. Jas., b.a., Bulmer Rectory, Welburn, York (2 copies).
Garratt, W. S., 19, Trafalgar Square, Ashton-under-Lyne.
Greig, Andrew, 36, Belmont Gardens, Hillhead, Glasgow.
Grantham, John, 2, Rothsay Place, Old Trafford.
Gillibrand, Dr., Parkfield House, Chorley Road, Bolton, Lancs.
Gilton, H. M., Cheadle Hulme.
Grafton, Mrs. J. H., Overdale, Altrincham.
Greenough, Richard, Church Street, Leigh, Lancs.
Grundy, E. A., Harthill, The Crescent, Cheadle.
Guest, Wm. H., Arlington Place, 263, Oxford Road, Manchester.
Garner, G., Rose Bank Works, Clayton, near Manchester.

Haggerston, W. J., Public Library, Newcastle-on-Tyne.
Hainsworth, Lewis, 120, Bowling Old Lane, Bradford.

LIST OF SUBSCRIBERS.

Hall, Joseph, The Hulme Grammar School, Manchester.
Hampson, Jonathan R., J.P., 4, Seymour Terrace, Old Trafford, Manchester.
Hampson, Fras., Platt Cottage, Manchester.
Harrington, Miss, Worden, Preston.
Heape, Charles, Glebe House, Rochdale.
Holden, Charles, 26, Sudbourne Road, Brixton, S.W.
Holden, J. W., 118, North Eleventh Street, Philadelphia, Penn., U.S.A.
Horton, Fred, Oak Guld, Malden, Surrey (2 copies).
Howorth, Daniel F., F.S.A. Scot., Grafton Place, Ashton-under-Lyne.
Howard, Dr., Altofts, Normanton.
Heslop, R. Oliver, 12, Akenside Hill, Newcastle-on-Tyne.
Hinton, Luther, Parkhurst, 228, Upton Lane, Upton, Essex, E.
Haslewood, Rev. F. G., Chislet Vicarage, Canterbury.
Hudson, John C., Durnlea, Littleborough, near Manchester.
Hudleston, R. J., 37 Cannon Street, Manchester.
Hall, James, Lindum House, Nantwich (2 copies).
Holme, Mr., Ravenoak Road, Cheadle Hulme.
Harris, Wm. Cowper, Editor, "Pembrokeshire Times," Pembroke.
Hoblyn, Richard A., F.S.A., 79, Priory Road, West Hampstead, N.W.

Jeans, Wm. Dampier, Sankey Warrington, Lancs.
Johnson, J. H., Auburn, Hesketh Park, Southport.

Kay, Thomas, Moorfield, Stockport.
Kaye, Cecil Lister, Denby Grange, Wakefield.
Keary, Peter, 15, Dent's Road, Wandsworth Common, S.W.
Kenderdine, Fredk., Morningside, Old Trafford.
Kirkman, Wm. Hy., The Star Bleaching Co., 22, Cooper Street, Manchester (2 copies).

Lamplough, Edward, Author of "Yorkshire Battles," Hull.
Law, William, Littleborough, Manchester.
Leader, J. D., F.S.A., Moor End, Steel Bank, Sheffield.
Leathes, F. de M., 17, Tavistock Place, London, W.C.
Lees, Samuel, Park Bridge, Ashton-under-Lyne.
Liverpool Free Public Library, per P. Cowell.
Lister, James, Rockwood House, Ilkley, near Leeds.
Lingard-Monk, R. B. M., Fulshaw Hall, Wilmslow, Cheshire.
Lilburn, Charles, J.P., Glaiside, Sunderland.

Maclona, Rev. H. Victor, M.A., Hilbre Grange, Bedford.
Man, E. H., 2, Palace Road, Surbiton, Surrey.
Manchester Free Library, King Street, per C. H. Sutton.
Mark, Ald. John, Mayor of Manchester.
McCormick, Rev. Frederic H. J., F.S.A. Scot., St. George's, Derby.
Midgley, Jas., White Horse Street, Leeds.
Mills, James, Beverley.
Miller, W. H., M.L.S., "Times" Office, Leek, Staffs.
Moon, Mr., Woodville, Bramhall.
Moore, Samuel, Moorelands, Weaste, Manchester.
Myers, Samuel Peel, 5, Colliergate, Bradford.
Midwood, Chas. H., Springfield, High Street, Oxford Road, Manchester.
Midwood, G. Norris, Portland House, Eccles.
Milne-Redhead, R., F.L.S., Holden Clough, Bolton-by-Bowland, Clitheroe.

Newbigging, Thos., 5, Norfolk Street, Manchester.
Nevill, Mr., Bramhall Hall, Stockport.
Norbury, Allan, Roslyn Villa, Oak Road, Withington, Manchester.

LIST OF SUBSCRIBERS.

Norcliffe, Chas. Best, M.A., Langton Hall, Malton.
Northgraves, Charles, St. Ann's Place, Manchester.
Nussey, Samuel L., Potternewton Hall, near Leeds.

Oldham Free Public Library, per Thos. W. Hand, Librarian.
Overton, Wm., 3, Lombard Court, London, E.C.
Ormerod, H., Boothroyde, Brighouse.
Oliver, Thomas, 8, King Street, Manchester.

Palmer, Wm. F., Park Mount, Higher Broughton (2 copies).
Parkinson, Mrs., Whitefield, Lymm, near Warrington (2 copies).
Price, Cornell, M.A., F.R.H.S., Westward Ho, N. Devon.
Pearse, Perceval, Sankey Street, Warrington (2 copies).
Pocklington Coltman, Mrs., Hagnaby Priory, Spilsby, Lincs.
Public Library, Belle Vue, Halifax.
Procter, Richard, Solicitor, Oak Mount, Burnley.
Phillips, Moro, The Long House, near Cowfold, Sussex.
Palmer, John Linton, Rock Ferry, Cheshire (2 copies).
Patchett, John, Mildred House, Undercliffe Lane, Bradford.
Platt, Owen, Prospecton, Greenfield, Oldham.
Price, F. G. Hilton, 17, Collingham Gardens, South Kensington, London.

Ramsay, P. J., The District Bank, King Street, Manchester.
Ramsden, Sam, Hightown Heights, Liversedge.
Radcliffe, Rev. John W., 38, East Southernhay, Exeter.
Randall, Joseph, Bank Chambers, George Street, Sheffield.
Renaud, Frank, Alderley Edge, Cheshire.
Rider, W. H., Little Hales, Leek.
Rivers, General A. Pitt, Rushmore, Salisbury.
Roberts, William, 95, Little Cadogan Place, London, S.W.
Robinson, Arthur J., Clitheroe Castle, Clitheroe.

Samon, Louis, Scotchwell, Haverfordwest.
Sanderman, Wm., Junr., The Chestnuts, Church, Lancs.
Shearine, Edward, F.S.A., 60, Gloucester Terrace, Hyde Park, W.
Simpkin, Edmund, Bury.
Simpson, Mr., Bramhall Park.
Smith, C. C., Limehurst, Knowle, Warwickshire.
Smith, David, 5, Cromford Court, Manchester.
Smyth, Albert H., 118, North Eleventh Street, Philadelphia, Penn., U.S.A. (3 copies).
Sotheran & Co., 49, Cross Street, Manchester (2 copies).
Southward, Henry, Ashleigh, Northen Grove, Didsbury.
Sugden, Mr., Park Road, Cheadle Hulme.
Stanier, Chas. F., "Examiner and Times" Office, Manchester.
Stephenson, John Watt, 1, Birch Grove, Rusholme, Manchester.
Stodd, Mrs. Sarah, Cross Street, Manchester.
Swaby, Rev. Wm. Proctor, D.D., Millfield Vicarage, Sunderland.
Swindells, Geo. H., 7, Cranbourne Road, Heaton Moor, near Stockport.
Swindells, Peter, Cheadle Hulme.
Subscription Library, Bolton, per J. K. Waite, Librarian.

Tadema, L. Alma, R.A., 17, Grove End Road, London, N.W.
Taylor, Rev. Edward J., F.S.A., All Saints, New Shildon, Co. Durham.
Tattersall, Wm., Quarry Bank, Blackburn.
Thornton, John, F. B. Welch & Co., Manchester Chambers, Market Street, Manchester.
Tinkler, Rev. John, M.A., Akengarth Dale Vicarage, Richmond, Yorks.

Thackray, Wm., 16, Hall Ings, Bradford.
Tolhurst, Jno., Glenbrook, Beckenham, Kent.
Threlfall, Henry S., 12, London Street, Southport.
Thompson, Joseph, Riverdale, Wilmslow, Cheshire.
Timmins, Saml., F.S.A., Arley, Coventry.
Turner, Wm., 128, Plymouth Grove, Manchester.
Tyars, John F., 20, Market Place, Wisbech.
Thompson, Fred, 1, St. Ann's Place, Manchester.
Tonge, Rev. Canon, M.A., 51, South King Street, Manchester.
Tuer, A.W., F.S.A., 18, Totting Hill Square, London, W.

Vaughan, Wm. Thos., 13, Adelaide Road, Brockley, Kent.
Venables, H. S., 28, Gracechurch Street, London, E.C.
Vickers, Allen, 28, Edithna Street, London Road, Stockwell, London, S.W.

Wallhouse, M. J., 28, Hamilton Terrace, St. John's Wood, London, N.W.
Walker, Rev. John, Whalton Rectory, Newcastle-on-Tyne.
Warburton, Samuel, 10, Wilton Polygon, Cheetham Hill, Manchester.
Watson, J., Oakfield, Cheadle Hulme.
Watson, W. A., 14, Newton Street, Manchester.
Wilson, James, Bookseller, Stratford.
Wood, Mr., Pauldens, Manchester (2 copies).
Wilson, William, J.P., 42, Glassford Street, Glasgow.
Wilkinson, Wm. King, M.A., Whiteholme, Slaidburn, near Clitheroe.
Winder, John Ed., The Villas, Bramhall, near Stockport.
Winterburn, Geo., Bookseller, 65, Deansgate, Bolton.
Whiley, Henry, Town Hall, Manchester.
Whitelegg, Thos., Water Lane, Wilmslow.
Wright, Jas. O., 32, Market Street, Bradford.
Wright, Samuel, Solicitor, 10, Piccadilly, Bradford.
Wright, W. H. K., Free Public Library, Plymouth.
Wood, R. H., F.S.A., Penrhos House, Rugby.
Woodd, Barie F., Conyngham Hall, Knaresborough.
Whist, John, F.S.A., F.S.I., 62, Old Broad Street, London, E.C.
Wurtzburg, Jno. H., Albion Works, Leeds.
Whytehead, T. B., Minster Yard, York.
Wilks, Matthew, Gorphwysfa, Old Colwyn, N. Wales.
Weeks, Wm. Self, Solicitor, Clitheroe.

WAKES AND RUSHBEARINGS.

THE DISAPPEARANCE OF OLD-TIME CUSTOMS.

[SPECIAL.]

"Many of our old customs are fading away into the dim mists of antiquity, and all but the name will soon be forgotten. This is much to be regretted, because they were attended with a great deal of pure enjoyment, and were looked forward to by the people for weeks before the event. One of these is the old custom of strewing rushes, and its attendant ceremony of rushbearing, with its grand rush-cart and fantastic Morris dancers. Once common to the whole country it now lingers in a few isolated places, principally in the hill districts of Lancashire and Yorkshire."

The above extract is from a volume on "Wakes and Rushbearings," published in 1891, under the editorship of Mr. Alfred Burton. It happily and exactly describes the moribund state of one of our oldest and merriest customs. The Wakes we have still with us. It is recognised as a general holiday in many parts of South-East Lancashire, and in some districts of Yorkshire, Derbyshire, and Cheshire. But even the Wakes of to-day is not what it was in olden times. It is shorn of the religious ceremonial of rushes, and the merrymaking time now runs on different lines, while the Morris dancers are not to be seen, or, if seen, they are mere caricatures.

* * *

The rushbearing ceremony, which usually brought the Wakes holiday to a close, goes very far back in our domestic history. In ancient times houses, even of great nobles, had no mats or carpets. The floors used to be covered with a plentiful supply of rushes. If guests of note came in clean rushes were strewn to add to their comfort. If no such attentions were paid the person was "not worth a rush"—a phrase in common use even to this day. Queen Elizabeth, it is said, was the last monarch of these realms who had her rooms strewn with rushes. As folks became more refined Oriental mats and rugs gradually took the place of our ruder floor-covering. Long afterwards, however, rushes were still used in churches. They made the bare floor more comfortable for the poor worshippers who had no cushions to kneel on; and at Wakes time every year these rushes were ceremoniously renewed. At first they were carried by the merry makers in bundles under the arm. Later this was not considered elaborate enough; and so ingenious Lancashire and Yorkshire folk hit upon a curiously designed cart known as the rush cart. It carried huge piles of rushes, and was gaily ornamented and made the centre of much pomp and ceremony. Here is a pen picture of it by Elijah Ridings, a Lancashire poet:—

> Behold the rush cart and the throng
> Of lads and lasses pass along!
> Now watch the nimble Morris dancers;
> Those blithe, fantastic sprite prancers;
> Bedecked with gaudiest profusion
> Of ribbons in a gay confusion,
> Of brilliant colours, richest dyes,
> Like wings and moths and butterflies.
>
> Behold the strong-limbed horses stand,
> The pride and boast of English land
> Fitted to move in shafts or chains,
> With plaited glossy tails and manes;
> Their proud heads each a garland wears
> Of quaint devices—suns and stars,
> And roses, ribbons—roughs, abound;
> The diver-plate, one hundred pounds,
> With green-oak boughs the cart is crowned;
> The strong gaunt horses shake the ground.

* * *

At a time when the Wakes holiday is in full swing in many parts of Lancashire, it is interesting to recall that in those far off times Gorton was "a village near Manchester, long celebrated for its breed of bull dogs, its sturdy men, and its wakes." The Oldham Wakes has a notoriety all its own; and so have the Wakes of Ashton-under-Lyne, Stalybridge, Stockport, and other places. About 1790, I gather from an interesting lecture by Mr. Hugh Dean, of Gorton, the rush-cart went out in Gorton on the Friday before the first Sunday in September, perambulating the village, visiting the homes of local celebrities, accompanied by bands and pikemen carrying staves, surmounted with brass eagles, and, of course, followed by an admiring throng. That same evening or on the following morning the rushes used to be teemed down near the chapel gates. The old ones of the previous year having been cleared out of the chapel the new ones were carefully strewn in the bottom of the pews, aisles, &c. The garlands which had adorned the rush-carts were also placed in the chapel. They were suspended on staves, which were fastened to the pillars in front of the lofts, where they remained till the next anniversary. On Sunday the Morris dancers and other officials connected with the rushbearing all attended the chapel, when an appropriate sermon was preached. This was the finish up of the Wakes, for labour was resumed on the Monday. This little account is typical of what took place in most places. The custom gradually died out, mainly because of the introduction of heating appliances and mats into the churches and chapels. So late as 1882 Mr. James Dearden, the lord of the manor of Rochdale, made heroic efforts to resuscitate the custom in that thriving and go-ahead town. He offered a prize of ten guineas for the best rushcart, five guineas for the second best, and a guinea to all competitors. That year Rochdale had a particularly gay Wakes indeed, but as the prizes were not offered again there were few rush-carts in the following year, and lack of appreciation in subsequent years practically killed the custom.

* * *

How many people, I wonder, could tell without turning up records that the Morris dance was brought to England in the reign of Edward III., when John of Gaunt returned from Spain. "In the dance," says Dr. Brewer, "bells were jingled, and staves or swords clashed. It was a military dance of the Moors or Moriscos, in which five men and a boy engaged; the boy wore a morione, or head piece, and was called Mad Morion." At the time this dance was introduced into England the tournament was still the first of sports. Bull baiting, bear and badger baiting, cock-fighting were the recognised Wakes pastimes. On Sundays and holidays, after divine service, the poor people went in for practising archery, which they were bound to do by royal proclamation. Money was extremely scarce in those days. The haymakers got a penny a day; labourers three halfpence; masons threepence; carpenters twopence, and so on. The people in each county were not allowed to go out of their own county for work, although the men of Staffordshire, Derbyshire, and Lancashire enjoyed certain privileges in that respect. The introduction of the Morris dance enabled the dancers and rushbearers to solicit money from the local gentry and with the proceeds make merry in the time honoured fashion—that is to say, they became exceedingly drunk and for the time being took all manner of liberties.

As the old Wakes customs died out others sprang up. In time the holiday became nothing more nor less than a fair. To a great extent it is a fair still. Where there is a Wakes holiday on there, you will find the market square or other convenient and centrally-situated ground converted into a show ground, the attractions being the merry-go-round, with mammoth musical instruments and penny shows. These penny shows are fearfully and wonderfully devised. They include ghost shows and primitive dramatic representations, menageries with performing lions and wolves, assaults-at-arms, picture galleries, the fat woman, the lean man, and other human curiosities, strength-testing machines, shooting booths, and among other attractions toy stalls, sweetie stalls, ice cream barrows, and similar things beloved of country bumpkins and juveniles. But just as these Fairs killed the old Wakes customs so they in their turn are being slowly killed by the superior attractions of seaside places such as Blackpool, Southport, New Brighton, Morecambe, &c.

* * *

Time was when holiday makers had no other option but that of staying in their native towns and villages, varied by occasional visits to Manchester, where they saw many unfamiliar sights and encountered many strange adventures. All that was changed when the railway companies found out the means of drawing away thousands of pleasure seekers into what was to them "fresh woods and pastures new." At first even railway travelling was expensive and could only be indulged in sparingly. Then those ever enterprising companies found that they could profitably take passengers for fifty and sixty miles and back for the small sum of half-a-crown. From that time to the present day new experiences and very delightful holidays came with the Wakes; and to meet the need for "pluto"—the newest slang term for money—the working population organised "going off" clubs. These clubs have taken root not only in public-houses but in savings banks, and in mills and workshops. Trifling subscriptions regularly made every week for months before the Wakes accumulate into tidy sums, and when the holiday comes thousands of pounds are taken for the sole purpose of spending in change of scene and pleasure. Our operatives and workers generally can thus afford very comfortably all the exactions of sea-side places and the expenses of travelling, etc. The change throughout is for the better, and picturesque as were the old customs we are well rid of them. M.

www.ingramcontent.com/pod-product-compliance
Lightning Source LLC
Chambersburg PA
CBHW031817230426
43669CB00009B/1169